Why I Climb

Why I Climb

Personal insights
of top climbers: Robbins,
Whittaker, Hill, Skinner,
Bonington, Lowe, and
23 others

Steve Gardiner

Foreword by
Dr. Charles S. Houston

STACKPOLE BOOKS

Published by
STACKPOLE BOOKS
Cameron and Kelker Streets
P.O. Box 1831
Harrisburg, PA 17105

Printed in the United States of America

10 9 8 7 6 5 4 3 2 1

First Edition

Cover photo by Steve Gardiner

Cover design by Tracy Patterson

Interior design by Marcia Lee Dobbs

Library of Congress Cataloging-in-Publication Data

Gardiner, Steve.
    Why I climb: personal insights of top climbers, Robbins,
Whittaker, Hill, Skinner, Bonington, Lowe, and 23 others / Steve
Gardiner ; foreword by Dr. Charles S. Houston.—1st ed.
        p.   cm.
    Includes bibliographical references.
    ISBN 0-8117-2321-6
    1. Mountaineers—Biography. I. Title.
GV199.9.G37   1990
796.5'22'0922—dc20   89-28618
[B]   CIP

To my parents,
Wallace and Lavone Gardiner,
with love

Contents

Foreword

In this confusing and frenetic world we need now and then to pause for a moment to ask why we are here, where we are going, and what we are achieving. Humans do the bravest, wisest, and most foolish things, often not knowing why. Steve Gardiner has persuaded some of the best and bravest to explain what leads them to climb. Twenty-four men and five women from twenty to eighty-nine years of age talked with Gardiner; his condensation of these interviews makes this a fascinating and unique collection.

The climbers certainly recognize a wide range of motives. Though most deny that climbing is dangerous, calling it as safe as driving a car, most still delight in "living on the edge," echoing Plato's "the unrisked life is not worth living." Though a few hint at Herodotus's "great deeds are usually wrought at great risk," they insist that they climb safely. Yet few deny the addictive thrill of danger. They enjoy (and some seek) the sweetness of fame and the admiration of their peers but deny this is a major motive. Some frankly acknowledge climbing as a good way to make a living, doing what they like best. Some like to be alone, to solo the most difficult climbs; others value team spirit and companionship. Not one mentions the fellowship of the rope, perhaps because hardware has blurred that bond.

Motivation for the first difficult rock climb of which we have any record was clear: Domp Julian went up Mont Aiguille in 1492 because he was ordered to do so by his king; he felt it necessary to summon three lawyers to testify to his success (and perhaps to save his head). A century later Dr. Conrad Gessner was determined to climb high hills every year for exercise and the delight this gave his spirit. George Mallory's irritated snap "because it's there" is the most often quoted reason and perhaps the most vacuous. The chapter "Mechanization and the Cult of Danger" in R. L. G. Irving's sensitive book *The Romance of Mountaineering* caustically foreshadowed, in 1935, the shape of today's climbing. With Geoffrey Winthrop Young's *On High Hills,* Irving's book should be a bible for all climbers.

There's a world of difference between feats of the past and today, but motives now are no clearer than those of Gessner and Domp Julian. Non-climbers can't understand the lure, and climbers can't or won't explain it. Competition, probably never absent, is more obvious and extreme today as are the material rewards.

It may be significant that the theme of this book is "climbing" and climbers: not "mountaineering" and mountaineers. This is not a semantic slip. A century ago the ascent of mountains by any route was a leisure activity, a refreshment and a game. Today the emphasis is on new and more difficult variants. Though a charming guide to roof climbing at Trinity College, Cambridge, written in 1907 reads much like today's guide to the Gunks, the goal then was to defy authority rather than gravity. The anonymous author wrote, "In these athletic days of rapid reversion to the Simian practices of our ancestors, climbing is assuming an ever more prominent position . . . the supply of unconquered Alps is naturally limited, and the dangers of Nature's monumental exercise grounds are yearly increased by the polish of frequent feet and broken bottles. . . ."

Although today's aspirants seek the extremes of difficulty on boulders, sheer faces, cracks or spires, the great peaks have not been neglected. Quite the contrary, there too the most difficult and dangerous routes are the prize sought by many. Everest may not have become Mummery's cow peak or an easy day for a lady, but its most dangerous and difficult faces and ridges are sought while the "ordinary" route may be followed by amateurs.

Many of those whom Gardiner interviewed were attracted by the thrill of discovery and exploration and the wish to see what's on the other side, to go where no one had gone before, but not so much to explore secret valleys as to reach untouched summits. A few (almost shyly) spoke of the beauty, the peace, the quiet, and the special beauty of great mountains; others were just as happy on the most difficult crowded cliffs near home.

Several expressed a wistful longing for the primitive life, for getting back to basics, a need to take control of their lives. Yet throughout the pages runs a thread of instant gratification, a sense of now, not later. Many spoke of success but did not try to define it; some equated success with style, with process rather than with outcome; others felt success in climbing had led to success in business and in making the right contacts. Not surprisingly the few older persons were more philosophical, even nostalgic for the way things used to be, but their juniors spoke only of today. Many enjoyed several sports, often those with other risks like kayaking in harsh waters. How candid they have been the reader must decide.

This is a revealing and provocative book, sure to be widely read and quoted, but unlikely to change patterns. At least it may prompt some people to look again at what drives them, look beyond today and tomorrow, and perhaps find in mountains more than climbing. They will recognize the wisdom of George Mallory, "Whom have we conquered? None but ourselves," and Maurice Herzog, "There are other Annapurnas in the lives of men."

Charles S. Houston, M.D.

Acknowledgments

In writing a book of this nature, the cooperation of a great many people is essential. First and foremost, I wish to thank each of the climbers who granted interviews and submitted photographs, often stacks of ancient album shots, to make the book possible. I would also like to thank the many people who suggested names, supplied addresses and phone numbers, or provided background information on climbers being considered.

Thanks to Chris Bonington for permission to use quotations from his book *The Next Horizon;* and the Sierra Club Books for permission to quote from Arlene Blum's book *Annapurna: A Woman's Place.*

Interviewing climbers without having a background in the sport myself would be very difficult. For this background and the years of happiness climbing has brought me, I want to thank Larry Yost, who took me into the Wind River Mountains for the first time; Charles Lee who drove me to the Lake District in Northern England to watch rock climbers; Frank Sanders and Terry Rypkema, who hauled me up Devils Tower one weekend and spent the next several summers teaching me to climb safely; Karl Ritsert of Germany, who shared climbs with me on three continents; Joe Sears, who was my partner in Alaska, the Tetons and many other places; Dave McNally, my tentmate on Everest; Rick Dare, teammate in Alaska and on Everest; Mark Brackin, who endured nightmare hanging belays on long aid routes; and Mark Higdon, Dallas Virchow, Doug Burbank, Ted Handwerk, Hans Meyer-Blankenburg, Christoph Lauterwasser, Dennis Horning, Chris Ballenger, Dick Guilmette, Gordon and Mary Ann Gildroy, and Dave Wood. Thank you all for sharing the challenges, dreams, and laughs.

Cam Patterson of the Tenton County School District and Nancy Effinger of the Teton County Library helped me locate research materials on countless occasions. Dr. Duane Grimme, Kim Stafford, Kevin Doll, and Katie Sears all provided inspiration to keep the writing going. Chet Fish of Stackpole Books believed in the book from the very beginning and provided several significant suggestions along the way. Mary Suggs and Ann Wagoner, also of Stackpole, made valuable editorial comments.

Special thanks go to Greta and Romney who, with their imaginations and observations, make a walk in the woods one of the greatest adventures in the world, and to Peggy, my ropemate for life.

Author, Steve Gardiner, with Buddhist monks in the Barkhor Market in Lhasa, Tibet, en route to Mt. Everest in 1988. **(Steve Gardiner)**

Why Climb?

We were camped on a saddle near the base of a beautiful mountain ridge that we intended to climb the next day. We were filled with excitement, anticipation. It was cold and still and thousands of stars filled the night sky. We talked on hour after hour about hopes, about dreams, about life. Someone asked, "If you could be anywhere in the world right now, where would you want to be?"

Nothing came to mind until suddenly I realized that I was already there. I was in the midst of wonderful mountains with good friends and a game plan for the morning.

"Come on, where would you want to be?"

"Right here," I answered. The whole scene was so perfect and, I realize now, so rare. It is not often that we, as human beings, are content with our place in life. But that night I was.

It was the first time, but not the last, that I felt that way in the mountains. It's not something that can be easily described, but the feeling was very real and very powerful.

Later, when another friend asked me why I bothered to climb, I tried to explain the emotions I had felt that night. I don't think I succeeded, but it did cause me to think more about what motivated me to climb. As with most climbers, I was asked the question on many other occasions and never really felt that I gave a good answer. Once I even tried to write down my reasons for climbing, but they didn't come close to what I felt.

Perhaps there isn't a good answer or perhaps there are many good answers. I decided it would be interesting to hear what others had to say and began searching for people who were willing to give an answer. I went to people I had read about, people familiar enough with climbing to have given the question some thought. This book is their collective answer.

It's not easy to find such people. I found some in campgrounds, on isolated backcountry trails, at sidewalk cafes and, when I couldn't see them face to face, on the other end of a telephone line. Their comments are as diverse as their personalities, and it is in this variety of who they are, of their ideas, and of their motivations that I found the real purpose of this book. It is not a book about climbing as much as it is a book about people who climb. Yet, at the same time, it is not a comprehensive biography of these people, but a collection of their feelings and beliefs. Most recount a memorable climb or two (and I've listed their climbing credits) as a context for the ideas and emotions they wish to express.

The book is not intended to be a climber's Hall of Fame, although the people who are represented here would surely qualify for such honors if they existed. Nor are these people the only ones capable of speaking on this topic. Another writer could easily find a roster of different climbers to fill a similar book. However, after twelve years of climbing and reading about climbing, I chose the people included here as the ones I most wanted to hear explain their motivations for climbing.

Since the purpose of this book is to explore why people climb, the reader, both climber and non-climber, will expect to find here an answer to this age-old question. One reader will find the answer in the first chapter, another in the middle of the book, and yet another at the end. For another reader the answer may be more of a puzzle, with pieces drawn from several chapters or all the chapters until they begin to interlock. In some cases, comments made by one climber contrast vividly with those made by another. In other cases, they are mirror images. It is certain, however, that when man mixes with mountains interesting things happen and thoughts about nature, religion, and the human mind, body, and spirit abound.

Scott Heywood

Born:

September 30, 1948, Kettering, Ohio

Hometown:

Sheridan, Wyoming

Occupation:

Owner, outdoor sporting goods store

Climbing Highlights:

First ascents of rock routes in Yosemite, Colorado, Canadian Rockies, Brooks Range, Alaska Range, Wind Rivers, Bighorns, Vedawoo, Snowy Range, and Garden of the Gods. Winter ascents of ice climbs in many of the same areas. Also, kayaking trips in China, Tibet, Alaska, and Wyoming

While a senior in high school, Scott Heywood went to Switzerland with his family on a ski trip. There he met a young man who was training to be a guide and went out climbing with him.

"It was really spooky," Heywood recalled. "It was obvious from my untrained state that it was dangerous, but it was also very exhilarating, exciting and involved a lot of energy. I was from Ohio, flat country, and never had any experience like that. It was unique."

After finishing college, he moved west and learned more about technical climbing. "From 1970 to 1978, I was intensely involved in it. I climbed well over a hundred days a year. When I was going to graduate school I would climb almost every day in the summer; it became very clear to me that I was much more interested in climbing than in graduate school. At some point I guess you have to accept that. I was going into my lab early in the morning and leaving at noon so that I could climb until night, and I was working out all the time. I was obsessed with it.

"The generation I grew up with in climbing came of age during the switch from big wall climbing in Yosemite to the short, hard, free, crack routes. We still did big walls, but the emphasis was on short, hard, technical routes. It was a very invigorating time because the standards were being raised dramatically. There was an explosion in climbing and a much different atmosphere than it has now. There are a lot more climbers now. 5.10 climbers are a dime a dozen now but then, if you were a 5.10 climber, you were really doing something. The psychological limits were really being pushed. It was a time when the Cookie in Yosemite was done, when the Steck-Salathe was free-soloed by Henry Barber, when Royal Robbins and [Yvon] Chouinard were coming down and a new generation was coming in. There was a switch away from a mountaineering mentality towards more of an alpine hard-core approach, where you really trained as an athlete instead of being an exaggerated hill-walker. That's carried through to today where most climbers get involved in one aspect of climbing, whether it be snow, ice, or rock and push their limits and then try to apply that to bigger mountains."

Heywood expects interest in climbing will continue to grow at a slow rate until it reaches a point where "it is somewhat like it is in England where a lot of people do it, where it is a very traditional competitive sport and people constantly come up with these little groups and strive for something different. It will become very tribal after awhile. It will be very difficult for people who can remember what it used to be like. It will be more and more technical because that is the only way it can go. A lot of the artistic areas have been explored. I don't think you're going to get much better than *Ascent* magazine, so it will probably become more of a mainstream American sport, which will be a little bit sad. It's sad when you see things turn into sports because then it becomes no different than basketball or football. If you become more interested in results and goals, it loses its process orientation and all you are interested in is product. It happens in fishing. You can see the same thing—a preoccupation with the technical side and a checklist to fish here and fish there and travel around. When I grew up, climbing was on the fringes and you had a personal input into the development of the sport. Now the sport is developed. It's big. It's changed.

"I have a very unique perspective on climbing now because I had a blood disease when I was a kid and had to take some drugs. As a result of that I've had a lot of injuries and physical problems and I've had to quit climbing for all practical purposes. I have a very distilled view of it now, of what's important to me about it, what I miss about it. So I'm not actively involved in it like I was, although my world still involves it through my business.

"I miss being up high, just simply the gain of elevation, the beauty, the view, the clear, distinct exact lines that things have at a high altitude. The air is thinner and everything is crisp and clean and pretty. There are so many things that you miss, the physical rigors, the fatigue at the end of the day. I miss being in exceptionally good shape. I miss that sense of commitment, that total involvement. I miss the opportunity, although I can get it somewhat in kayaking, to immerse myself in climbing and completely block everything else out. I think that's one of the advantages of climbing and one of the more meditative aspects of it. You can totally concentrate on a three-foot section of rock. No way you can think about anything else. In that way it's cleansing and I miss that.

"The things that I don't miss are sort of curious. I don't miss the ego aspects of it. I don't think about climbing hard things. To me now, to participate would be enough. To do a route that would push my abilities, and I don't know what they would be now, but to be on that edge is what I miss. I don't really care about the—for want of a better word—macho aspect of it. When people are doing it, it's very important, you know, the sense of accomplishment, and the feeling that you're really neat. I don't need that anymore. I think a lot of that stems from insecurities. Maybe people that are driven to climb really hard are insecure people, but I don't miss that. I miss the pure, wholesome aspects of it. When people are talking about climbing, yes, it would be nice to get in there and list my accomplishments along with theirs, to do the climbing rap, but I don't miss that. In fact, it's nice sometimes to walk away from it now and not feel compelled to get in there in those oh-so-subtle ways that climbers are so good at, because you know what you've done and in what style. To participate is what is important."

After he quit climbing, Heywood still wanted to be involved in an activity with some excitement. He took up kayaking. "With kayaking, I know I'm not going to be great. I know I'm not going to be anywhere as good a kayaker as I was a climber because I just don't have the physical attributes I had. But I have to have a sport where I can take some chances and draw some narrow lines. For example, how does it differ from basketball? Because you have to commit to it. You have to take a chance. When you go out onto a basketball court, you don't think, 'I wonder what's going to happen?' But you do have those moments in climbing.

"In kayaking you don't make conscious decisions as much. When you've started a rapid, you are committed and you have to do it. In climbing you make a conscious decision to go on constantly. You are much more in control. You can be sloppy at kayaking and get through. You make a mistake in climbing and you're going to get into trouble.

"I find that for me, to take charge of my life, to take a chance, to take a risk, is very important. It might be in business—we've got a business here. It's eight years old. We could go on ad infinitum and make a reasonable living, but it gets pretty boring if you don't take some chances, take some risks and see where you can take it. I would say that's also true in climbing. You make conscious decisions to take a chance, and when you take that chance you take control of your life, and when you take control of your life it has lots of benefits for you. It's confronting your fears head on. It's confronting a lot of human fears, fear of death, fear of falling; confronting things like laziness, inertia and being totally responsible for yourself, which is uncommon in our world today, and I think that's why I like it. It's immediate gratification. It gives you a sense of self-worth. It may be an illusion, but it's an important illusion."

According to Heywood, the real reasons for climbing are internal. "When I got obsessed with climbing, I was sort of goaless, purposeless. Climbing gives you a reason to be. It gave me a purpose and however arbitrary those definitions are, we were working at it very hard. I see that with young kayakers now. They are literally paddling to give their lives some purpose. I mean we're all so damn alienated. I think I was searching for something that would give me a sense of aesthetics, a sense of importance. It's like screaming in the dark, 'I'm here.' Those days are a frightening time in a person's life. It's almost like people who get involved in cults. It gives them a sense of purpose."

The learning that a climber experiences is also valuable; Heywood contrasted it with learning in school. "All through your education you have been forced to learn things that have no meaning in your life, but, dammit, everything you learn in climbing is important: knots, rope handling, everything. I remember when I was first climbing and reading magazines and how-to books on climbing; none of it seemed like work. It was something I just did. It was discovery education—Carl Rogers at his best.

"I started reading *Mountain* magazine. My first one was number 12, that's how long ago that was, and I can still remember how I absorbed that stuff. I was fascinated with what it would feel like to be up there on that mountain and looking down. I wanted to know what that felt like. I wanted to be an alpinist. I wanted to look like them. I wanted to have that gear. I wanted other people to know I was one of them.

"I can remember very clearly when I first did the North Ridge of the Grand Teton, which for many years was considered the hardest climb in North America. It was really important to me because it's very long, very committing. We had a spectacular bivouac on the Grandstand, an absolutely clear, beautiful night. We had to chop a little ledge out of a cornice up there to sleep in. The climbing was called 5.7, but it was that alpine kind of 5.7 with ice-choked chimneys and the leads were often unprotected. We came off the mountain in a very bad electrical hailstorm and we just ran down the peak. That was our first taste of the true, classical alpine ascent and it was pretty exhilarating. We were pretty high after that.

"On another climb in the Tetons, we thought we were on The Snaz and we ended up on a thing called the Pillar of Death. We ignored slings where other people had obviously rapped off. It turned into this 5.10 horror show and I remember standing on this ledge and we all were laughing. I said, 'Peter, this is the most frightened I have ever been in my life.' We didn't know where the hell the route went. It went up and dead-ended in this roof. We went up under the roof, traversed left, and it all opened up and we were able to finish the route. When we got down, Peter and I gave each other a hug and I hugged Peter's girlfriend, who had been down sitting by the stream during all this, not knowing what was going on. It was this spontaneous moment like, 'It's really good to be here. It's really good to be alive.'

"My climbing reminds me of my father's stories about World War II. Those guys will tell you that it was a horrible war and that it was tough and men were killed, but it was the best time of their lives. It was the highest energy. They can't stop talking about it. It made more of an impact than anything else in their lives, and though I think if you really got down to the root of it, they may not choose to do it again, they are sure damn glad they did it. I think it's a peak moment in your life. Why were those men willing to accept the risk in World War II? There was peer-group pressure, which we certainly have in climbing. It is so important to you to achieve the goal that you are willing to sacrifice anything. That's probably stupid, but humans do lots of stupid things. There's no way you can say that, in order to climb the Black Ice Couloir, it is worth it to risk rockfall, avalanche, all these things, in order to do some tongue of ice on some mountain, except that the rewards from it in our screwed up little minds seem worth it. And somehow in our genetic makeup we have this desire to achieve, to adventure. It gives you a peak in your life. That feeling justifies the risks.

"When I look back on the things I've done, I would like to do some of them again, but it would be a lot harder for me to do them now because I'm more aware of the fragile nature of life. I'm more aware that I'm going to die. I'm getting older. When you are young, you are immortal. You accept the risk without quite realizing what it is. You don't think there is a chance that you are going to die.

"If you fall and the rope catches you, you certainly have a moment of fear and it drives it home. Maybe what we want is to have the fact that we are alive driven home in us. Maybe what people search for is the fact that they are alive. You are out of the routine. You are not going through a day-to-day, mundane existence. It cracks you open. It jolts you. It gives you fear. Fear is a very distilled emotion. It's pure. It's like love. When it happens, it's an eye-opener."

Rick Ridgeway

Born:
August 12, 1949, California
Hometown:
Ventura, California
Occupation:
Writer, photographer, filmmaker
Climbing Highlights:
American Bicentennial Everest Expedition, K2 (first American ascent), Minya Konka (China), Vinson Massif (Antarctica), peaks in Peru and Mexico

"My mother sent me to Outward Bound as a high school graduation present, and she has regretted it ever since," said Rick Ridgeway. "I met some other climbers there and we started getting into it. I was smitten."

Ridgeway, who grew up along the ocean in California, attended the University of Hawaii "principally to major in sailing." He met another student who had a thirty-six-foot sloop and, after finishing his freshman year, he and four others sailed off in the boat for Tahiti.

"None of us knew much about sailing," he recalled, "but somehow after three weeks and 2,300 miles of open ocean, we made it. It was paradise found."

After that, Ridgeway spent three consecutive years climbing in Peru where he learned the rudiments of snow and ice and how to deal with altitude. He met several climbers and was invited on various trips, the biggest being the 1976 American Bicentennial Everest Expedition.

Although he did not reach the summit, the expedition was successful and he learned two important things. "It became obvious to me that the most essential quality for a Himalayan climber is not technical ability, but patience. Also, the Everest trip was a big influence on what happened to me later. I started working with the camera crew and that got me launched into a whole new series of adventures. I was working with a camera crew one day and it dawned on me that we were all doing the same thing—climbing the mountain. There was one difference, however. These guys were getting paid for it. This big light bulb came on in my head and I said, 'The movies are for me.' I talked with Mike Hoover and he gave me some tips. He was then and, without a doubt, still is, America's foremost adventure cinematographer."

Hoover suggested that Ridgeway think up an idea for an adventure film. Ridgeway remembered reading a passage in *Travels to the Americas* by Baron von Humbolt that described rock towers rising out of the jungle in South America.

"I thought it would be fun to try to climb some of them," Ridgeway recalled.

"After some research, we found one that sounded attractive because it had a 2,000-foot wall all the way around it, and there was a cave just below the summit that went all the way through the mountain like the eye of a needle. There was a rumor that some dinosaur creature lived in there and it came down at night and raided villages and ate babies. It sounded like good television to me so I told Mike about it and he wrote the proposal, sent it off to ABC, and pretty soon we were off."

The nine-day climb and the film were both successful, and that led them to more adventures. They filmed George Willig climbing in Zion National Park for ABC's *Wide World of Sports* and a ski mountaineering trip on the Forbidden Plateau in Antarctica for ABC. For this they used ice-climbing techniques to ascend floating icebergs and, pulling their sleds behind boats, claimed to be the first people to water ski in Antarctica.

Ridgeway was also involved in filming a movie called *High Ice* for NBC. "I was supposed to push a plunger to blow up a helicopter on a cliff. The charge was stronger than I expected and I lost half my moustache."

By 1978, K2, the second highest mountain in the world, had turned back all five American attempts to reach its summit. Jim Whittaker decided to lead a new expedition and invited Rick Ridgeway to join, both as a climber and author of the expedition book *The Last Step: The American Ascent of K2.*

"We were on the mountain for fifty-five days before we could make a summit attempt," explained Ridgeway. "We split into two summit teams. [John] Roskelley and I were wading in deep snow. [Jim] Wickwire and [Lou] Reichardt made it to the top by their route, so Roskelley and I traversed to follow them. Wickwire wanted to take pictures on the summit, so Reichardt left the summit first. Wickwire ended up spending the night out alone so Roskelley and I thought we were on a body detail. We passed Wickwire on his way down and he was doing okay. We reached the summit at 3:30. It was a day of high atmospheric pressure so that assisted us in making the no-oxygen ascent.

"People ask why I climb mountains and one of the reasons has to be what happened when we returned from the summit. Wickwire, as tired as he was, got himself up and started a stove to brew some tea for us. I'll never forget that. It was a great gesture."

In 1980, Ridgeway was a member of the second American expedition allowed into the newly opened mountains of China. He was on Minya Konka with Yvon Chouinard, Kim Schmitz, and Jonathon Wright. The four were caught in an avalanche (also recounted in this book by Chouinard) and fell more than 1,000 vertical feet.

"Everybody was injured," said Ridgeway. "Kim had cracked his back in two places and Yvon had a concussion. Half an hour after we stopped falling, Jonathon Wright died. We buried him at the base of the mountain and turned our backs and went home.

"The rug had really been pulled out from under me. I wasn't sure if I ever wanted to go on another expedition again. I really put a lot of thought into whether I wanted to continue taking those risks. I realized some of the things I had gotten out of it, particularly the friends I had made. Staying in there for sixty-eight days on K2 really taught me to stay with a project until you got where you were going. But the biggest lesson of all was the avalanche because when I was going down I thought I was dead, so every second was as valuable as it could be. You had to wring out everything you could. I wasn't panicked. It was like I had fifteen seconds left and I had to really make them count. Then it stopped and I had millions of seconds in front of me and I was rich. I had the ultimate wealth. Those are the kind of things that you couldn't get anyplace else."

When Dick Bass and Frank Wells set off on their attempt to climb the highest peak on each of the seven continents, they asked Ridgeway to go along. He was on three of the climbs (Aconcagua, Everest, and Vinson) and wrote a book about the quest (*Seven Summits*).

"This all started out as an interest in an offbeat sport. In high school, I was attracted to the eccentricity of climbing rocks. It sounded like it would be fun to do and I always felt a bit like of an outsider and an outcast character. I was also attracted to travel. I love to think about foreign countries. I love to read about them and I developed a passion, not just for foreign countries, but for very remote areas. Climbing on remote mountains just seemed like a great combination of interests.

"I found there were a lot of other outcast sorts of characters and that became a big part of it—the camaraderie of fun people and the travel to remote and exotic places. Then I learned about the thrill of completing a big ascent, of having to teach yourself to push your body and learn the skills to safely get up and down these mountains. That was satisfying. I felt like I had really accomplished something personally.

"I have made my living out of these adventures. There are three ways to do that. You can be a guide, like a lot of my friends are; you can be in the equipment business; or you can go into the media end of it. I've done all three. I've found, in trying to make my living out of writing and making films, that I'm getting more and more interested in writing and filmmaking for their own sake and I would love to be a better writer and filmmaker. I'd love to make documentaries and write more, both non-fiction and fiction. That's a big goal for me now, equally as big as my dreams used to be of reaching the highest summits.

"I love to launch off on a project that, at the outset, doesn't seem too likely to succeed. Those are always the most valuable when you look back on them. Those are lessons you learn from the mountains. It seems trite perhaps, but in completing some of the projects I've done in the last few years, I've paused when I've gotten frustrated and thought to myself, 'Wait a minute. This isn't any harder than getting up K2 and you hung in there. You didn't think you were going to make that and everything turned out fine.' People learn those same lessons in other ways. Businesspeople have their own K2's."

Ridgeway is a father and because of that admits, "I'm more conservative and cautious now. It's fine. It's a natural progression and it doesn't mean that I'm going to quit climbing or going on adventures. I think that going out on day climbs is one of the greatest thrills of all. I love that kind of thing.

"I want to encourage [my children] to be curious. I think that's the most essential ingredient for a vital life. If I can give them that, I think I'll have succeeded. It was a curiosity about mountains, climbing, and foreign places that got me started. That was the basis of my initial interest. If their curiosity leads them to other places, that's fine."

James W. Whittaker

Born:
February 2, 1929, Seattle, Washington
Hometown:
Port Townsend, Washington
Occupation:
Former president, outdoor equipment business
Climbing Highlights:
Everest (first American ascent, 1963), K2 (leader of first
American ascent, 1978), Everest (leader, 1990 International
Peace Climb), Rainier (sixty-six ascents), numerous climbs in
Cascades, and many others

As the first American to climb Mt. Everest and the leader of the first American expedition to climb K2, Jim Whittaker has been an important force on the two highest peaks in the world.

Whittaker became interested in climbing Mt. Everest in 1952 when he read about the Swiss expedition. Then, the following year, he was guiding on Mt. Rainier when he received news that Hillary had reached the summit. It was another ten years before he got his chance to go but, as it turned out, it was worth the wait.

"I knew that it would be the hardest thing that I would ever do so I trained very hard for it," Whittaker said. "I was in top shape when we left. I weighed the same after the 185-mile hike as I did at the beginning of it so I did not lose a pound on the approach."

Whittaker was ready mentally as well as physically. "They interviewed the whole team at the Office of Neural Research. They said I was the only one of the nineteen that said, 'Yes, I will get to the summit.' I guess I was pretty confident of it. I thought that if Hillary could do it, I could do it. I was quite strong and powerful. Professionally I had logged a lot of ascents from sea level to high altitude and I'm sure that helped my lung capacity."

The expedition was nearly cancelled when Jake Breitenbach was killed in the Khumbu Ice Fall. The team members discussed the future of the expedition and decided to try to finish the climb. Throughout the ascent, chronicled by James Ramsey Ullman in *Americans on Everest*, Whittaker remained strong and enthusiastic. His experience in the Mountain and Cold Weather Command and his sixty-six ascents of Mt. Rainier as a guide apparently helped, as his prediction that he would reach the summit proved true. At age thirty-four, Whittaker walked onto the summit of Everest and into the history books, but the significance of the moment was not immediately impressed upon him.

"A lot of people ask me what I thought about when I was on top of Everest and my classic answer is what [Nawang] Gombu, the Sherpa that climbed with me to the summit of Everest, said at the first press conference in New Delhi when they asked him what he thought about when he was at the highest point in the world—'How to get down.'

"The winds were still over sixty miles [per hour] at the South Col, we were both out of oxygen, and the temperature was thirty-five below zero, so we spent barely fifteen minutes on top and started down. As a result, we didn't really think much. Even at high camp, I didn't feel a sense of accomplishment because we were out of oxygen and we had to survive the night. It wasn't until after I had come back through the ice fall that had killed Jake that I really relaxed and experienced a surge of relief and fulfillment. I was worried about the ice fall. I had a feeling that maybe the mountain was going to get me now for having stood on top. I felt more vulnerable having done the top. I went through [the ice fall] unroped and running fast. I knew everyone would be going too slow for me."

Only after clearing the ice fall and making sure that all the team members were safe did Whittaker feel the thrill of his accomplishment. Even in his moment of joy, however, he did not realize how great a change the event would make in his life.

"I got a lot of recognition. I met President Kennedy in the White House and got an award from him [the National Geographic Society Hubbard Award for exploration]. That led me to meet Bobby Kennedy; I led him up the highest unclimbed mountain in Canada, which was Mt. Kennedy, named after the late president. I got involved with their family and skied with them at Sun Valley and in Colorado. I was campaign manager for him in '68 and ran his campaign in Washington state. I was with him when he was killed in California. That had quite an impact on me."

During this time, Whittaker was president of Recreational Equipment, Inc. (REI) and the business, which had been doing well, started growing even faster. By 1978, REI was large enough to become a major sponsor for the American K2 Expedition and Whittaker would be the climb leader.

"My goal going over was to lead a successful expedition to the summit of K2. I had climbed the highest mountain in the world. If I could lead an expedition to the second highest mountain, I would have fulfilled two goals."

The expedition ran into problems with weather and later with dwindling supplies. After more than two months on the mountain, a last minute break in the weather allowed Jim Wickwire, Rick Ridgeway, John Roskelley, and Lou Reichardt to become the first Americans to reach the summit.

"We were very lucky to get that mountain. We almost didn't get it. We were low on supplies and were pretty wasted. We had been high for about seventy-six days and didn't have much power left. I thought we could do it, but we had already tried once and failed. Success is sweetest to those who have known defeat."

Having experienced success and death of friends in the mountains, Whittaker is keenly aware of the risks involved. "It's unfortunate that mountaineering lingers on the fine edge of tragedy, but it does. I suppose that's one of the excitements of it. I've always felt that a person who lived a little bit close to the edge lived a little bit more aware. You have heightened awareness at those times and are more aware of how good life is and appreciate life more than someone who hasn't experienced the delicate nature of it."

Whittaker described his reasons for climbing mountains. In the Cascades near his home he climbs "because I have such a strong love of nature that I think that being in nature in the mountains or at sea or in the wilds, is the most true and real experience a human being can have. Nature, to me, is all-powerful and all-true and fair and gives me the closest touch that I could have with any creator. It gets me back to my roots when I'm in nature. I am more comfortable outside than inside, and outside cities than inside cities. I much prefer nature."

About mountains like Everest, where nearly one climber has been killed for every two that have stood on the summit, Whittaker explained, "At those odds you have to justify it for other reasons, although it is very beautiful over there and the majesty of the mountain is great. To seek that challenge is the core and mainspring of all human activity. If there's an ocean, we cross it. If there's a disease, we cure it. If there's a record, we break it. If there's a mountain, we climb it. I believe in that. It's meeting challenges. God knows there are a lot of mountains in one's life."

More than twenty-five years after his brief stay on the summit of Everest, Whittaker still receives letters from schoolchildren who have read about him in history books. He enjoys answering their questions about mountain climbing. "I like to pass on my knowledge. As I get older, I have mixed feelings. I've lost a lot of good friends in the mountains, but I feel that if people are careful and can take care of themselves, in many ways it's safer than seeing how fast you can drive in your vehicle."

For Whittaker, concern for safety is paramount in the mountains, but that does not necessarily mean replacing experience and judgment with additional equipment. "I think some of the equipment is superfluous. As an equipment manufacturer, I suppose there is some jeopardy in saying that, but I think there is some overkill in the gadgets that people think are necessary to go into the mountains. I hope to see a trend where climbers will go lighter and take less technical equipment with them. They can enjoy it more if they are closer to the rock and doing things more like we used to do with balance climbing. I would, however, encourage people to get out; that's what the thread of my life essentially has been. The out-of-doors is where people should be. I think they're more human there, more natural. There are vast amounts of knowledge to be gained from nature, so I would encourage people to enjoy it. I guess my philosophy has been that the mountains are dangerous, but don't let the danger stop you from going there, from doing what you want to do. They should be gone into, sat around, stood on, and contemplated. There is a lot of strength that can be drawn from that experience."

Whittaker likes a special quote from John Muir, which he recited from memory: "Climb the mountains and enjoy their good tidings. Nature's peace will flow into you as sunshine into flowers. Streams will bring you their freshness and storms their energy, and cares will fall off like autumn leaves."

Richard D. "Dick" Bass

Born:

December 21, 1929, Tulsa, Oklahoma

Hometown:

Dallas, Texas

Occupation:

Oil and cattle business,
owner and developer of ski resort

Climbing Highlights:

Matterhorn, Aconcagua, Kilimanjaro, Elbrus, Vinson, Kosciusko,
McKinley, and Everest; first person to climb the highest mountain
on all seven continents. Oldest man, at fifty-five, to climb Everest

"I popped out of the womb with blanket curiosity, hyperenthusiasm and non-stop verbosity," said Dick Bass. "With those traits, I naturally had a nickname in high school—Large Mouth Bass."

And it was his verbosity that got him started on a climbing career at a time in life when most athletes are retiring. Bass and some employees at his Snow Bird Ski Resort in Alta, Utah, were talking about a possible climb on Mt. McKinley. Bass expressed an interest in going. His only other experiences with mountains were a guided ascent of the Matterhorn in 1949 (inspired by the books of Richard Halliburton) and a climb up Mt. Fuji in Japan while he was on leave during the Korean War.

Bass still wanted to go. He explained, "Marty Hoey, who was a guide on Rainier and McKinley, looked at me and said, 'Bass, your hot air ain't gonna get you up that mountain.' I was going to show her, but I quickly learned that I was dealing with Superwoman."

Within six months, a ten-member team from Snow Bird was on McKinley carrying seventy-pound packs and hauling thirty-five pound sleds. "I never dreamed I was going to get up it," Bass confessed, "but ringing in the back of my mind was Hoey's comment. I was so mentally determined you could have stuck a knife through me and it wouldn't have fazed me."

Under Hoey's leadership, the climb went well. Bass was one of the summit climbers. "I stood on top at fifty-one years of age. I gave my Tarzan yell. I felt like gangbusters. Back in camp, Hoey came over to me and gave me a big bear hug. She said, 'Bass, I don't believe you. You're an animal.' I swelled up like a bull elk in rut."

After the McKinley climb, Bass got an idea. He had just climbed the highest mountain in North America. Why not climb the highest mountain on each of the seven continents? Hoey thought it was a good idea and asked to go along with him. Bass mentioned it to a business friend and not long after the friend called and wanted to introduce Bass to Frank Wells, president of Warner Brothers since 1972. Wells had climbed Kilimanjaro, the highest peak in Africa, in 1955 and had developed the same dream but had not followed through because of his career. The two men met and decided to pursue the seven highest mountains together, a journey they called the Seven Summits Odyssey.

Since both had difficulty being away from their careers, they decided to try to climb all the peaks in one year. They set up practice climbs on Aconcagua, Elbrus, and Rainier. Bass, who has a resting pulse of forty-one, reached the summit on each one, but Wells had some difficulty. They decided to make the arrangements for the seven climbs anyway and enlisted several top-name climbers—Rick Ridgeway, Chris Bonington, David Breashears, and others—to accompany them.

McKinley (North America), Aconcagua (South America), Elbrus (Europe), Kilimanjaro (Africa), and Kosciusko (Australia), were all successful ascents with relatively few problems. Even Vinson (Antarctica) went well after they were able to work through the opposition of several Antarctic Treaty nations. It was, as might be expected, Everest (Asia) that presented the most trouble and caused the seven-summit quest to extend beyond one year.

In a period of thirty-eight months, Dick Bass spent twelve of them on Mt. Everest engaged in four separate expeditions. A 1982 expedition on the North Face was a particularly difficult one for Bass as his friend Marty Hoey, who had challenged him to climb McKinley in the beginning, fell to her death.

Undaunted, Bass returned the next year with a Norwegian expedition. "When I left for Everest, my wife told me to remember three things: 'Never let your guard down, remember how much you have to come home to, and I love you.' "

Twelve days after leaving base camp, Bass was on a summit attempt. He was climbing unroped above the Hillary Step and ran out of oxygen. "I felt like I was going to drown," he recalled. "I was so tired. I just wanted to let go, but, in my mind, there was Marty Hoey saying, 'Come on, Bass, you're an animal.' "

That's when Bass pulled out his "secret weapon." "Whenever the going gets really rough and I'm exhausted and can't breathe and can hardly keep going, I just recite one of the many poems I have memorized. I have a poem for every occasion. I think they are helpful because of the rhythm. I get lost in it and march up the mountain.

"Those poems give me a secret weapon most people don't have. I learned on McKinley that I could say these poems and keep positive, and positive thoughts are what you need to keep going. I can lock into a poem like a mantra."

It must work, because Bass did reach the summit of Everest at age fifty-five, the oldest man to do so, fulfilling his dream of reaching the seven highest summits.

"I'm not a great technical climber. I was getting on-the-job training on all these mountains. I'm a peak bagger, not a first ascenter. If I'd latched onto climbing when I was a teenager like Breashears, I would have done very well."

He may not be a technical expert, but his desire has more than compensated for anything lacking in his climbing background. "I failed three times on Everest, but I didn't stop trying. Climbing these mountains reinforced convictions I had before. I have a greater appreciation for the blessing of life than I have ever had. I don't care how much the bankers are on me, or the regulatory officials, or anyone else. No human-induced pressure is going to cause me to lose sleep anymore or knot up my belly. I am so thankful to be alive. Climbing Everest doesn't give you a big head, it gives you humility. On the summit, I dedicated the climb to Marty Hoey and said a prayer of thanksgiving. Now, when I have a problem, I don't say, 'Why are you doing this to me?' but 'What do you want me to learn?' And I'm going to keep going, too, because I'd rather wear out than rust out.

"These mountains have given me a philosophical strength that I don't know what else could have given me. When it's hour after hour of having your tail puckered up to your tonsils, it gets indelibly ingrained. Now, when I start to get uptight, I can say, 'Wait a minute, Bass, you're here and you're alive.' When I think of what it was like up there on the summit of Everest, everything else just falls away. I don't let it knock me out. I don't think anything is ever going to be more of a challenge, in terms of fear and daring and stamina, than what I did on the summit of Mt. Everest."

Even before the Seven Summits Odyssey, adventure was important to Dick Bass. In 1979 he took his four children, three of whom had already graduated from college, on a five-month trip to experience the "hopes and fears, joys and sorrows within each member of the human family on the spaceship of Earth." They climbed the Matterhorn and Mt. Olympus, ran the course taken by Pheidippides from Marathon to Athens (which they finished by running a lap around the Olympic stadium holding hands), swam the Hellespont, scuba dived to 240 feet, and walked the Milford Track.

"The story of my life is a giant leap into the unknown," said Bass. "There are things that we are inclined towards. I'm inclined to be an adventurer."

"I am not a contentious person, but I am very competitive. All you have to do is throw down the gauntlet. If somebody tells me I can't do something, I want to do it all the more. Everyone tells me I was crazy to climb Everest. I owed money. I had a family. But I've always had an adventurous spirit and I've learned that to live is to participate. Spectators only exist.

"I have a strong faith, a personal faith. I'm praying everyday. I don't mean a prayer asking for things, more a prayer of thanksgiving, and I want to show my appreciation by being a good person."

Everest might be the tallest mountain in the world, but for Dick Bass, there is a mountain that is bigger—Snow Bird Ski Resort in Utah. He is developing the resort and, once again, trying to bring dreams into being.

"I've lost over thirty million [dollars] to Snow Bird," he admitted. "That's pretty adventurous. I think Everest was God's way of getting me into condition to finish this Snow Bird deal. It's not going to be easy."

Some friends once gave Bass a silver bowl. On it was carved the saying, "The greatest use of a life is to spend it for something that will outlast it."

That "something" for Bass is Snow Bird, not only the ski area and hotel, but a concept he calls the Snow Bird Center for Human Understanding, which would house the world's foremost library of climbing books and films.

"The Center for Human Understanding is where all these other things were leading me. I'll have a convention center, conference center, performing arts theater, health center, nutrition center and mountaineering center. I'll canvass the world for people who are at the cutting edge of human understanding, give them a room, and have them teach anything and everything man is trying to do. Every Saturday I'm going to have a whole new potpourri of leaders from around the world. What a spark-flying setting that will be.

"I got this idea from the mountains. I'll make as little a footprint on nature as possible. The facilities won't be obtrusive. All the buildings will be in easy walking distance of each other so cars won't be necessary.

"It will be a place for getting honest with yourself. If you can't be a friend to yourself, you can't be a friend to your fellow man. I'll have teachers come in with scholarships for a week or two. I believe teaching is the greatest calling in the world and what these school teachers learn can help foster self-respect in young minds. If children learn self-respect, they can learn other things on their own. Malcontentedness stems from a lack of self-respect. Ninety-nine percent of the way things happen to us we make happen in our minds.

"I've already lost a lot of money on this; I don't like to lose money, but I know it isn't the end of the world. In our western thought, if you aren't always going forward, that's a negative. In the oriental philosophy, they have yin and yang, and the negative is just as important as the positive. An oriental looks at a hammer and knows that when the blow is spent, the hammer must retreat. Just pushing the head after the hammer hits won't do anything. It has to retreat to strike again. This is how I look at my work. I give my best lick and if it doesn't work, I don't panic. I back off and get away from it, and it comes. Or like [Rudyard] Kipling said, 'Meet triumph and disaster and treat those two imposters just the same.' I'll keep after this project. I've got enthusiasm for this. That's why I have the energy. I don't just have second winds, I have third and fourth winds. Everest got some of my doubters to start believing me."

Bass believes in the power of the mind and its potential. To keep his own mind ready to deal with the pressures of climbing and business, he created several "Bassisms."

"One of them is, 'Don't ever have just a few problems. Always have a bunch because that way nothing gets blown out of proportion.' Another is, 'My dreams of the future sustain my present agonies.' "

The Center for Human Understanding is not the only dream left for Dick Bass. "I'm going to get a great big boat, maybe a hundred-footer, with air compressors so I can go scuba diving anywhere in the world. I'm going to have a grand piano on there, and I'm going to have my easel. I'm going to paint, play my piano, write poetry, and read all the books I've wanted to read but haven't had time to read for the past twenty-five years. I'm going to go around the world and sail the seven seas. I'm going to study the world's waters. I spent the first half of my life doing the have-to's so I'm going to spend the rest of it doing the want-to's."

Jan Bien Conn

Born:
April 22, 1924, Takoma Park, Maryland

Hometown:
Custer, South Dakota

Occupation:
Private music teacher, lecturer, musician

Climbing Highlights:
Over 250 first ascents of spires in the Needles area of South Dakota, first female ascent of Devils Tower National Monument, many rock climbs in New England, and exploration and mapping of more than fifty miles of passages in Jewel Cave National Monument

"I think we climbed out of our cribs and just kept going," remarked Jan Conn about herself and her husband Herb. "We knew each other as kids and often scrambled around on the cliffs in New Hampshire. That's where we learned to love climbing. I remember seeing a couple of climbers up on a cliff in Franconia Notch when I was a kid and, gee, I wanted to go join them so bad. At that time we just scrambled without ropes, but during the Second World War we were in Washington and managed to contact this zany group of climbers on the Potomac River. The cliffs were low, but the standards were high and we learned to use ropes. After we had been climbing technically, we went back to New Hampshire and realized that we had been climbing things we probably shouldn't have [without ropes]. Anyway, it always seemed really natural to climb.

"We had been bumming around for three or four years and were kind of looking for a place to sink some roots. We saw those spires up there [the Needles], and they looked so good that we figured this was the place to do it.

"It was easy for us to climb first ascents here. There are so many summits. Usually we just looked for the easiest way up and climbed it. Our routes aren't as hard as the things they are doing today, like Freak's Foot, but we sure had fun.

"We would finish a climb and be sitting on top, trying to think of a name to put in the register. I remember watching big black thunderheads rolling in while we were thinking up names, before we would skitter down the thing. We left registers on each of the summits and some of them have survived and some of them haven't. We used little half-pint paint cans and coated them with aluminum paint to try to keep them safe, but the lids would rust shut and people had a terrible time getting into them, I guess. The ones on the more frequently climbed summits have been replaced. Every now and then, somebody will find one of our old registers. A lot of them, I think half of them, had to be bolted to the summit. The summits were so small that you couldn't build a cairn to bury them in. Sometimes the wire would break and some of these registers have been found lying in the grass at the bottom of the pinnacle."

Jan and Herb, who worked as a professional climber for fifteen years filling cracks in the faces on Mt. Rushmore, kept close records of their climbs over the years and even mapped the areas in which they were climbing. "Herb made his own little transit. We took it to all the summits and we took readings on all of them. In fact, the Mystery Spires got their name because, from certain places around Sylvan Lake, they stick up and look very much like the Cathedral Spires. We thought we were seeing the tops of the Cathedral Spires, but they just didn't line up right on his map. We didn't know what they were so we called them the Mystery Spires.

"Station 13 is the name of a spire up there and that was the thirteenth station in our survey of the Needles. And it was kind of a thirteenish type of climb. In the Cathedral Spires where the pinnacles seem to divide themselves into groups, we numbered them Spire One, Spire Two, up through Nine for the main groups. Different summits within the group could be almost anything. Fred Beckey came here and did two first ascents. He called them Rubaiyat and Khayyam. From that, we took the Moving Finger, the Tower of Darkness, and the Shaft of Light, which are all quotations from the Rubaiyat. Then we got into another area where there is a pinnacle that starts as two and then joins, and we called that The Tuning Fork. Beside it there is a little point we called The Sharp, a flat-headed one we called the Flat and another called the Heck of a Note. Some of the names fell into categories like that."

Being among the earliest climbers in America, the Conns often had to make adjustments. "We started climbing with a sixty-foot rope," Jan explained. You aren't going to get very far on a rappell with that. We started climbing down as well as up, which used to psych everybody out. We never understood these climbers who think that you can't climb down. If you can't climb down, what do you do if you are climbing up and the route becomes unclimbable? I know a lot of the protection we put in was with the thought, 'I know I can make this step up, but I've got to come down it last, so I think I'll just put in a piton.' You don't mind so much on the way down if you are groping for a foothold and you've got a piton there. We always felt it was easier climbing down, because you've got gravity working with you instead of against you, and if it's fun climbing up, it's fun climbing down. I think a lot of people get into trouble when they continue up because they don't think they can climb back down.

"We normally did climb with a rope. Not many people encouraged solo climbing. In fact, it was kind of a no-no and back east there was a reason for it. You were climbing in an area where every Boy Scout and his family could come by with their picnic lunch and if they would see somebody wandering up a cliff, they might not even realize that it was technical climbing. Climbing without a rope sets a bad example. However, one day we decided to climb all the numbered spires in the Cathedral Spires. That's a lot of climbing to do in a single day, so we did quite a bit of that unroped, just using the rope here and there for the pitches we didn't feel as good about.

"Another thing we got into the habit of doing back east, where you have only low cliffs, was doing traverses. We spent one summer, when we weren't near any rocks, doing that on a railroad underpass. Everyday we'd go out to this underpass and try to figure out the moves to go across it. It was terrific climbing. We never did get across it without falling off because your fingers would get so tired. The technicalities of working out those moves always appealed to us.

"That reminds me of another traverse we did, too. In my home just outside Washington, D.C., we had a heavy oak dining room table. It had an unusual system of legs that supported it, and we figured out our Dining Room Table Traverse. You had to start at one end of the table and go all the way under through this network and come up on the other side without touching the floor. My dad was rather dismayed at these carryings-on. Herb and I had both done this and one day a fellow came to the house and said, 'What I want to see is this Dining Room Table Traverse.' My dad figured that we were asinine kids that hadn't grown up yet. Then this dignified, educated man perches himself on the dining room table and does this complicated crawl through it. My dad just couldn't believe it. It was fun to realize that you could grow old without having to go through this nasty business of growing up. In fact, we're ready for our second childhood now."

Climbing was a chance for the Conns to get away and they seldom saw anyone in their large playground. "There was a time when, if we saw anyone in Custer who had skis on the roof of their car or who was wearing cleated boots, we knew we would have company that evening. It was such a small fraternity. If they had climbed two or three of the Needles and seen our names on top, we knew they were going to look us up. Years later, it was strange to see people walking around in cleated boots and realize they weren't anybody we knew or," she added with a laugh, "wanted to know. It was very satisfying to be a part of developing climbing in the Needles, but now it seems like it was somebody else."

Mentioning the cleated boots brought back memories of early climbing footwear. "When we started climbing, the best shoe we could find was a cheapy sneaker we bought for $1.99. We used to kid that we could take them back a month or two later and say, 'These are faulty, because they have a hole right here,' " she said, pointing to the ball of her foot and laughing, " 'and everything else just looks beautiful.' From that, they went to the really stiff mountaineering boots, suicide shoes we called them, and then they gradually got back to a more and more flexible type of cleated boot. Now they've come back to just almost exactly what we were buying for $1.99."

Herb and Jan Conn kept up a steady pace of climbing for seventeen years. "Some people don't ever reach the saturation point," Jan explained, "like Fred Beckey and Fritz Weissner, but we had enjoyed it enough." That didn't really mean the end of climbing for the Conns, though, just a change of venue. They moved from the rocky spires of the Needles into the depths of the unexplored Jewel Cave. This led them to twenty-two years of underground climbing and the publication of their book *The Jewel Cave Adventure*.

"It's a funny thing," she observed. "With all the climbing we did, I don't think we ever gave a talk on it. Somehow it didn't appeal to us. We don't like to take pictures. I think it's because the emphasis is on 'Look what I did.' Even though that may be the reason that a person climbs, it isn't anything that you feel particularly good bragging about. With the cave, it's different. You're exploring a world and you are introducing that world to the people who come to hear the talk. You aren't talking about what you did, you're talking about the cave. A lot of the movement is like climbing, maneuvering your body in cracks and chimneys, but the emphasis is different. In climbing, it is a challenge to see how hard a move you can make, but in the cave your whole purpose is to get to the extreme and as easily as you can, using as little energy as you can, so the emphasis is on the cave, rather than on the people who happen to be in there.

"Hand in hand with the exploration of the cave is the mapping. It's a very time consuming, exacting, mathematical type of affair and a lot of people who go climbing and caving don't want to mess around with reading compasses and making sketches. They want to explore. They want the excitement of it.

"Our whole life has revolved around climbing and caving. All those years. One thing that amazed us was that, when we were doing it, it was so all-absorbing that we felt that, even when we were too old to climb physically, we would still be tied emotionally to the Needles, and would be interested in everything that happened there. That hasn't been the case. When we started caving, we spent very little time in the Needles. Caving is going to be the same way. Right now, we're still involved in it, and in the summer we still take people in to see things. We still have more of a familiarity with the entire cave than the young fellows that are doing the work now. They know their way from the entrance to where they are working, and they know the new parts that they are working which, of course, we don't know, but we still have an awful lot of knowledge of the cave that we explored that probably no one else will ever have. They aren't exploring it. They simply take the easiest way through it and go to where they are working."

The Conns have evoked both criticism and praise for choosing the lifestyle they did. "People who knew Herb figured that, when we got married, he was really twisting my arm to make me do all these unladylike things. People who knew me were wondering how on earth I found anybody who would do all these things with me. I think my mom would have been happier if I had married a person who was a little more normal. She thought that I was strange enough without marrying someone that would pull me to be even stranger. I think Herb's mom was disappointed that he didn't use his engineering education, but I think most of that was just at the start, before everybody realized that we were doing all right in our own peculiar way. We didn't have the standards that other people had. The strangest thing is that by doing what you really, very selfishly, want to do, if you just go at it and do it with everything you've got, you end up making some kind of a contribution. It's completely unintentional. For the caving particularly, we have received some awards and things and all we were doing was rooting around and having a ball."

Exploring the two worlds of the Needles and Jewel Cave has given the Conns a lifetime of enjoyment. But Jan pointed out one personal conflict. "There's a contradiction in the cave. We did an awful lot of that exploring—just the two of us. You're torn. You discover something and you want to show it to other people and yet, when you actually do take someone into a part of the cave where you've been the only people, it loses a little of its charm. You're always torn between the desire to show it to people and the desire to still have that feeling about it. We've always argued that the cave or the passage belongs to the person who explored it.

"I can remember, as a little kid, going up to a tree and planting my feet right up against the trunk in the hopes of standing where no one else had ever stood. I told this to my mother and she thought I was nuts, but my dad said, 'I used to do the same thing.' I think it's something that's either in you or isn't in you. This was one thing that kept us climbing and is one thing that keeps you going in a cave, too. Even more in a cave. Anybody can look at a rock climb, but you can't even look at a room in a cave until you go there. When you are exploring you know, as you walk down the passage, that your light is the first light that has ever fallen on that rock. I think pioneering is the common thread that runs through both the climbing and the caving for us." And then laughing she adds, "We're still looking for something that old and decrepit people can do. Somehow raising hybrid roses doesn't have the same appeal. Although in some ways it's the same and I sometimes get excited about it. People have got that spirit. I mean, think of the guys who went to the moon. Can you imagine looking up there and thinking, 'I've been there'? It's the thing that keeps the human race progressing. I'm not saying that they progress very much when they are climbing or caving, but it's that feeling of new frontiers. I know that when I write a song I get the same feeling. But I think it has an extra kick when it's physical, too."

Bradford Washburn
Born:
June 7, 1910, Boston, Massachusetts
Hometown:
Belmont, Massachusetts
Occupation:
Honorary director of the Boston Museum
of Science, cartographer, photographer
Climbing Highlights:
Climbs in the Alps in 1926, 1927, 1929, and 1931, including
Arete des Rochassiers (first traverse), Col du Plan (first ascent of
Chamonix Face), Aiguille Verte (first ascent of North Face), and
Dent du Requin (second ascent, South Face). Climbs in Alaska on
Mt. Bertha (first ascent), Mt. Hayes (first ascent), Mt. Steele
(second ascent, first traverse), Mt. Lucania (first ascent), Mt.
Marcus Baker (first ascent), Mt. Sanford (first ascent), Mt. Crillon
(first ascent), and Mt. McKinley (third, fourth, and sixth ascents
overall, and first ascent of West Buttress route). Produced maps
of the Grand Canyon, Mt. Kennedy, Mt. McKinley, Mt. Everest,
and the Presidential Range, New Hampshire

When Canadian climber Walter Wood reached the summit of Mt. Steele in
the Yukon in 1935, he looked toward the summit of Mt. Lucania, the highest
unclimbed peak in North America. He saw how the saddle between the two peaks
dropped more than 2,000 feet. For the first time he saw the ten-mile gap between
the two peaks. He imagined making that traverse after the difficult approach he
had just finished to climb Steele and came to a conclusion—Mt. Lucania was
virtually inaccessible and unclimbable.

"No climber should ever say that," Bradford Washburn said. "Immediately,
Bob Bates and I said, 'Let's do it.'

"None of us really knew about the environs of Lucania because it is so far
back in there. It is behind Mt. Logan on the Alaskan side and, on the Canadian
side, you can't even see Lucania because it's behind Mt. Steele."

Washburn and Bates, along with Russell Dow and Norman Bright, decided
to use a different approach than Wood. They hired famed Alaskan bush pilot Bob
Reeve to drop them on the Walsh Glacier at the base of Lucania. That required
a glacier landing at 8,700 feet, a trick never before accomplished.

Reeve made three successful landings in May 1937 to establish an equipment cache. On June 18, Reeve took off with Bates and Washburn and made another high altitude landing.

"We were dumped in there with the theory that Reeve would take us out again when we were through, but the landing was a sea of slush, if you can imagine it at that altitude in Alaska. He barely got out of there with his life and said, 'I'm not going to bring your two companions in here and you two are just going to have to find your way out on foot.' "

They had brought along several waterproofed aerial photographs of the surrounding area, taken by Bradford Washburn in 1935, and knew the shortest way out was via the Walsh Glacier. However, having just flown over it, they also knew that route was in terrible condition and much too dangerous for a party of two. The only other way lay over the summit of Steele—the same situation Wood had envisioned, only in reverse.

Setting up a series of eight camps, Bates and Washburn made the climb of Lucania on July 9 and returned to the 14,000 foot saddle between the two peaks. From this camp, leaving much of their equipment behind them, they made the easy ascent of Steele on July 11 and that night were at its base at the head of Steele Glacier in the Yukon. With the climbs of Lucania and Steele behind them, Bates and Washburn planned to follow much of Walter Wood's route out to civilization.

"When you are that age (I was twenty-seven and Bob was a year younger), we were perfectly confident that we were somehow going to get out. We didn't have any question about it. We felt that trying to walk out the one hundred miles into Alaska to McCarthy was too dangerous. I would have liked to do it, but I didn't want to cross all those big holes with just the two of us. We were, I suppose, naively confident about getting across the Donjek River. We talked about getting some driftwood and making a little raft, but the driftwood was all on the other side of the valley! We didn't have an axe or a saw, so we decided it was easier to walk fifteen miles up the Donjek River and cross on the glacier where it was smaller. We must have gone about thirty-five miles out of our way to go a couple of hundred yards."

The exhausting journey left them without food. When Bates shot his pistol at a squirrel, he hit the branch it was sitting on instead. The squirrel fell off and was knocked out. Their first meal. One rabbit and a lot of mushrooms were the only food they could find until they came upon a pack train that took them on to Burwash Landing on July 19. They flew out the next day.

Washburn recalled an incident that gave him great pleasure. "In 1935, *Life* magazine had run a story about Steele being climbed. They used wonderful pictures and said Lucania couldn't be climbed. I had the delight of going into the managing editor's office and saying, 'Here is an article from two years ago saying Lucania is unclimbable and here is a batch of 8 X 10 glossies that show you how we climbed it.' "

In 1942, Washburn and Bates were together again—this time on Mt. McKinley. Even though there was no map at that time, Washburn had made the first photographic flights over the mountain in 1936, so they had copies of his aerial photos.

They were part of a team testing cold weather equipment for the Air Force, and were to spend two weeks at 17,000 feet. Washburn and Bates were friends of Belmore Browne, and wanted to see and record exactly where Browne had been stopped by severe storm conditions just short of the summit in 1912, barely missing the first ascent of the highest peak of McKinley. Washburn, Bates, and five others climbed to the summit and took pictures of where Browne had turned around, a spot only ten minutes walking from the summit on a clear day. They took the pictures and gave them to Browne. "He was absolutely thrilled," Washburn recalled.

The climb of Washburn and Bates on the U.S. Army Alaskan Test Expedition in 1942 was the third ascent of the peak. Washburn came back in 1947 for the fourth ascent with his wife Barbara, his climbing and mapping partner for over four decades. She became the first woman on McKinley's summit. Washburn returned again in 1951 on the sixth ascent. This was the first ascent of the West Buttress route, which is now considered the standard route on the mountain.

"It is very interesting to see that just as soon as somebody does something, then more people do it and more people do it and there have now been well over 5,000 ascents of McKinley! That's incredible.

"As you dissect a big mountain or a mountain range, you start out doing the first ascent generally by the route that is shortest, safest, easiest. The amusing thing about our West Buttress climb on McKinley was that it had to wait for all those other ascents before somebody did it and, of course, it is the safest, shortest, and easiest. There's a reason for this. It is on the 'back' side of the mountain. It would have been very complex and costly to get into that country and go all the way up the Kahiltna Glacier without knowing that the climb existed. We found the route from the air in 1936 and didn't get onto it until 1951. We knew it was there, and when we looked down on it from Denali Pass in 1947, we knew it would be short and safe if you were landed on the glacier, but if you added on another fifty miles of walking, that would thin down the hundreds of climbers that do it each summer now.

"My point is that you first do the easy things, usually a ridge because a ridge is safer. Then you do something more difficult until you get to a point where all the salient and safe approaches to a peak have been done. Then people begin to say, 'Why don't we try the face between those two ridges.' That face hadn't been climbed yet because—I won't say it was dangerous—it was less safe than the ridges that flanked it. People naturally want to continue to do something bigger and better than the other guy. The choice of things to do that haven't been climbed, and that are safe, is getting cut down to an awfully small number. For example, the only big climb that hasn't been done on McKinley is the East Face. I've sent pictures of that around to a number of top climbers who wanted to try it. One group went up the ice fall and came down saying their route had been swept by avalanches a number of times, rather like the Khumbu Ice Fall [on Mt. Everest]. What happens is you get into more and more climbs that not only involve enormous technical competence, but in addition to that, are getting more dangerous. My generation was lucky to be able to do wonderful virgin climbs that were pretty damn safe."

Washburn had a unique beginning to his climbing career. "I got into climbing because I wanted to avoid something else, which is a very unusual way to get involved in anything. I had paralyzing hay fever and I discovered inadvertently that when I was walking in New Hampshire and I got above about 4,000 feet, there was no hay fever."

That was the start, but other motivations quickly took over. There were four hard seasons in the Alps doing climbs that were the standard of their day. Then there were the Alaskan climbs, the aerial photography, and the precision maps.

Washburn explained, "There was a book called *Passages* [by Gail Sheehy], which emphasized the fact that there are periods in your life. I had a very active period of climbing when we were in the Alps and on Mt. Crillon in Alaska. Then there was the mapmaking and climbing period. As my museum work overwhelmed me, and I couldn't get away and was getting older, I got more and more into the business of photographing and mapping. I got an enormous amount of vicarious pleasure in taking pictures from the air and locating routes I would have liked to climb if I were twenty years younger. Then I would write an article for the *American Alpine Journal* and sit back and see what would happen. Soon after, somebody would want to go and climb one of those routes. I'd have more fun writing back and forth with them and giving them pictures with which to make the climb. I'd suggest where I would have gone if I had done that route, and then it was fun to see if they did what I would have done.

"When you're climbing and you know what is going on in the mountains, you have your own private little routes and you're not going to tell anyone else what you're thinking. By then I knew I couldn't do any of these climbs so I keenly enjoyed revealing my ideas, one by one. You get wonderful letters from these people thanking you for being a catalyst in what they did. I guess this was my Catalytic Period," he remarked with a laugh.

"Then I got really busy with maps. It began with the McKinley map in 1961, then Mt. Kennedy, and the Grand Canyon. You see, I'm moving away from actually being *on* mountains, but still working with really rough, exciting country. I did the 'field work' for the Mt. Everest map when I was seventy-four and didn't do any climbing at all. We used NASA, and its shuttle photography, to evaluate what was accurate and what was unreliable on the remarkable old maps of the British, Chinese, and Austrians.

"I've always enjoyed getting out into the wilderness. I happen to be very interested in mapmaking and photography, and getting into and over big mountains is what lent great excitement to mapmaking and photography. It was a way of getting out into virgin country with a bunch of neat fellows and it was always fun, then, to share our experiences with other people, to bring back photographs or make a map so that other people could go into this same country more easily and at less expense.

"The thing that was important to me was not just the business of going up the mountain, but of being on the ridges and looking out and looking up and looking down. The climbing was just a way of getting there. It was a means to an end, the end being to get to these wonderful places with great people and sit around camp, shooting the breeze, eating sardines, boiling kidney beans, and sharing the dreams. The thing that is exciting to me about the trips is not what you do, but who you do it with. It's a people business rather than a thing business."

Mapping the big mountains was a major part of Washburn's life. At Harvard, he developed a fascination for glaciers and a desire to make exact maps of their movements. This interest got him into contact with Swiss mapmakers, a connection that has been significant throughout his life.

"Without the Swiss, we couldn't have done any of the good maps we have done," he explained. "They are experts in producing the final draft of a map, the photogrammetry of it."

The original idea of an Everest map first came to Washburn in 1936, but the equipment and technology weren't ready. By the 1970s, however, aerial surveying had been refined to an art, and Washburn spent nearly ten years putting into place all the people and permits he would need to actually produce the Everest map. Using photographs taken by the Columbia space shuttle in 1983, and those from a Learjet flyover in 1984, Washburn directed a team from ten nations in producing the most exact map ever produced of the world's highest mountain.

"We took the photos on December 20 and 22 because, by that time of year, the mountain is blown clear of the monsoon snow. We had 165 miles of wind and 63 degrees below zero at 12,000 meters, but inside the Learjet everybody was in shirt sleeves."

The quality and quantity of his work in cartography and photography, and his accomplishments as director of the Boston Museum of Science for forty-one years, have earned him numerous awards, including honorary doctorates from Harvard and the University of Alaska, an Explorer's Medal from the Explorer's Club, New Englander of the Year Award from the New England Council, Engineer of the Year Award from the Engineering Society of New England, the Alexander Graham Bell Award from the National Geographic Society, and awards from the American Congress of Surveying and Mapping, the Royal Scottish Geographical Society, and others. The National Geographic Society, as part of its centennial celebration, brought together a distinguished group of members for a special evening. Both the Washburns received Centennial Medals at a dinner that Washburn insists, "will never be duplicated. Barbara and I have known a lot of those people very well. We've known Hillary for thirty years and have known Jane Goodall since 1970. Richard Leakey and his mother we've known for years. This was a real old homecoming."

The years have been busy for Bradford Washburn. If anything, they are just getting busier. In his seventy-eighth year, he saw the publication of two maps— those of Everest and the Presidential Range. "It was a frantic year," he said. "We had manuscripts going back and forth all the time."

Washburn, who has a Belmore Browne painting of Mt. Crillon at the foot of his bed, has devoted a lifetime to the mountains as climber, photographer and mapmaker. "People like to be on the pioneer fringe in whatever they are doing," he explained. "Some people have asked me why I'm still doing this. I tell them I like to be on the cutting edge of the twilight of life."

H. Adams Carter

Born:
June 6, 1914, Newton, Massachusetts

Hometown:
Milton, Massachusetts

Occupation:
Retired school teacher, editor of
American Alpine Journal

Climbing Highlights:
Nanda Devi (1936, first ascent, and 1976), K2 (1973 reconnaissance). Leader of fifteen expeditions to Peru including climbs on Yanacaico Norte (first ascent), Tumarinaraju (first ascent), Jatungarabanzu (first ascent), Milpocraju Chico (first ascent), Paccharaju (first ascent), Churihuauqui (first ascent), Yahuarraju (first ascent). Member of Alaskan expeditions to Mt. Foraker (second ascent, new route), Dagelet (first ascent), Mt. Crillon (first ascent), and others. Winter traverse of St. Elias Range (1935), climbs in the Alps, Rocky Mountains, and New England

Little was known about the region around Nanda Devi in the Himalayan mountains of northern India when the 1936 British-American Expedition set out. Adams Carter was a member of that team, which entered the Nanda Devi Sanctuary, and was on the team that made the first ascent of the highest peak in the British Empire.

Forty years later, Carter was on another Nanda Devi expedition. This time it was with Everest West Ridge veteran Willi Unsoeld and his daughter, Nanda Devi Unsoeld, who tragically died on her namesake mountain during the ascent.

"In 1936, we walked from the foothills," Carter explained. "It was a much longer approach, but that was a real privilege, because the people were—I won't say without contact with Western ways—but they were still very much the way they had been for a long time. In 1976, the people had had more education and it was very interesting to see the contrast between the two times. For example, in 1936, we wanted the porters to come back and get us after a month so we gave them so many pebbles and told them to throw one away each day and when there were no more pebbles, we wanted them in base camp to help us back to the outside world. In 1976, we said come back on the fifteenth of September, or whatever the date was.

"It was interesting to see the country again and see how much I remembered. It is a fairly complicated approach. I came to a ridge and said, 'I remember exactly what is on the other side of this from forty years ago,' and it would be exactly what I thought. Of course, it would be a place where the route was a little complicated and so it had been ingrained into me.

"The one thing I didn't do to the same extent in 1936 was to talk to the people. I did much more of that in 1976. I found that the first time I didn't know enough to ask the right questions. Forty years later, that was one of the things I found very interesting."

Although both expeditions reached the summit of Nanda Devi, Carter talks little of this. He has been more interested in the exploratory aspects of expeditions, and that interest got him involved in a daring and difficult winter traverse of the St. Elias Range in the Yukon, in 1935.

"It was the last blank spot on the map of North America," he said. "Brad Washburn got National Geographic interested in supporting us on that expedition. We started off with the idea that we were to produce a map of that region, which we did. That was our primary objective, which often interfered with the climbing. We left in February when the crevasses were covered and it was easy to move around on the glaciers. We discovered three or four glaciers that were over forty miles long. We learned that the Hubbard Glacier was ninety-two miles long. People hadn't realized that it was anywhere near that long. We also turned up a number of very high mountains.

"I had never experienced such cold weather for so long a period of time. For ten days, the warmest it got was forty below and often it was as low as fifty-six below. We spent an awful lot of time in our sleeping bags trying to figure out how you could read and hold onto your book. It was tough, because you didn't want to have your hands out of the sleeping bag. I was sharing a tent with Bob Bates and he would read the left hand page and the right hand page of the book out loud, hand the book to me, and put his hands under the sleeping bag. I would read the next two pages out loud to him and then give him the book so he could read to me again. We got a lot of good reading done that way."

Carter, who taught languages at Milton Academy for thirty-four years, has climbed peaks all over the world. Yet his greatest contribution to the sport of climbing has taken place in his own home, where he has painstakingly edited the last thirty annual editions of the *American Alpine Journal*.

"When I get too senile, they'll make me stop," Carter joked. "One of the troubles is that I've kind of worked myself into a corner. I've made an awful lot of contacts all over the world. Many people send me material without me having to prod them. I have to write letters in five different languages. I find if I write in English to a German, Italian, Frenchman, or Spaniard, I may not get a reply, whereas if I write to them in their language and they know they can reply in their own language, it's much more likely to produce results."

Hundreds of letters are required for each issue of the *Journal* and Carter writes each one, often sending a second or third letter if the initial account is not complete.

"I have two advantages in terms of making details as accurate as possible," he said. "Since it is a yearly magazine, I don't have to face the pressure of deadlines so often. Also, I have been in many of the regions that are being written about. I can question a bit more than somebody who hasn't been to many of the ranges of the world."

When Carter was teaching, he spent many Sunday mornings with his students rock climbing near his home, or ice climbing in New Hampshire. During this time, he also became interested in programs for exchange students, which led to interest in climber exchanges.

"I think it is very important to have climbers of different countries in contact with each other. It is interesting to see differences in techniques, but what is even more important is the improvement in international relations. It is just a drop in the bucket, but if you put it all together, it does help international relations. In most cases, climbers are intelligent people who can influence other people's thought. As a consequence, I think that if relationships between climbers are good, that might rub off on international relations in general.

"I think that very often people think that if that's the way it's done in Concord, New Hampshire, then that's the way it's done all over the world, and they don't realize that you've got to have a great deal of flexibility in your thoughts. There isn't a norm in many aspects of thought. I think that by foreign travel and contact with foreign people, you acquire more tolerance and realize that there are many things you can learn from them, and things they can learn from you."

Carter was the captain of the ski team at Harvard for two years, competed, as a member of the U.S. Ski Team, at the World Championships in 1937, and was captain of the U.S. Ski Team at the 1938 Pan-American Championships. This background, combined with his climbing experience, led him to a civilian job with the military intelligence in World War II. "Much of the work I did had to do with mountain warfare," he explained. "I was investigating what our allies were doing and what the enemy was doing in mountain warfare and how it applied to the Americans. Today if you mention intelligence, everybody thinks that you were doing dirty tricks, but it wasn't that. It was gathering information on all phases of mountain warfare. Along with that, I was developing equipment and finding out what our allies and the enemy had for equipment. Some of the time I was in the U.S. and some of the time I was in the field. I had the distinction of having a pretty interesting time and, as a Quaker, not having to bear arms. What I did, I had a feeling, was very useful, but did not involve me being an active soldier."

Climbing has literally been a life-long activity for Carter. When he was five, his father took him up Mt. Washington and, by the time he was fifteen, the family took a trip to Europe. "We had a great time climbing the Matterhorn when all the local guides said it was out of condition because of too much snow," Carter said. "My father, mother, a sister, and I all made the climb. That, and other ascents, was my introduction to the big mountains.

"My first expedition was to Mt. Dagelet on the Alaskan panhandle. We had an expedition of six, and four of us, Bob Bates, Charlie Houston, Brad Washburn, and I still see each other frequently and are very close friends some fifty-five years later.

"That's one of the marvelous things about climbing—the friends you make. I think climbers have closer relationships to other people than almost anybody else, because you do forge friendships of that kind."

Carter has slowed down on his climbing now that he is in his seventies. "I perhaps wore out my hips carrying too many loads. I've got two artificial hips. Lately, I've found that if I was leading, I'd want to bring my foot up somewhere near my chin and I don't bend that way anymore. As a consequence, I've decided that it is probably a bit foolish to do much leading now."

Still, he has kept up with the developments in the sport. "I shudder when I think of some of the climbs that even today are considered to be pretty good ice climbs and we did them with an ice axe belay, driving the pick of the axe in and putting a rope over it, which probably wouldn't hold anything. Now you can do it much more safely, so I think you can do much more difficult climbs than previously.

"One thing we felt was that there should always be a margin of safety. If you were in the big mountains, you ought to have a certain amount of food that could get you down in case of a storm. Nowadays, it strikes me that you try to cut the margin of safety as fine as you can. I'm sure that part of the fun of climbing is coming home again and reminiscing, having your memories about it. I suppose this is an old fogey attitude, but I think of some of the very difficult climbing that is being done under extreme conditions and it strikes me as Russian roulette. I'm not deploring what they are doing. I admire it, but I question it for me.

"I think in a few cases, it's unfortunate that people have sponsors now and have to produce something spectacular. I'm not sure that this spectacular business is adding what I think is the right thing. If you have to climb up Mt. McKinley backwards, with your hands in your pockets, blindfolded, and moving only in the hours of darkness just to say you are the first person to do it, it seems to me somehow foolish. Like the media show on Everest where they had to fly off it with a glider, and had to see if they could climb Mt. Everest in twenty-four hours from base camp—I think that somewhat cheapens the sport."

Carter, who has been a member or leader of more than thirty expeditions, remembers the early explorations in Peru when only two or three teams made climbs in a year. On one trip there, their climbing expedition suddenly became a rescue mission.

"In 1970, there was an earthquake that killed 67,000 people. You don't go and climb mountains when people are dying right and left and suffering, so we changed the nature of the expedition and took in doctors and nurses. They gave us the back side of the Cordillera Blanca, the eastern side. There was no lack of doctors and nurses who wanted to go, but most couldn't get around in the back country. Our doctors and nurses could.

"Another thing that we did in South America was follow up on a report that Ojos del Salado was higher than Aconcagua. We went down to make an accurate survey of how high it was in 1956. Unfortunately, we couldn't make it more than the second highest in the Americas, but we did find out just how high it was and did a first order survey of the peak. Our altitude has been accepted as the official altitude for the mountain."

In the end, though, climbing for Adams Carter is usually equated with camaraderie with his teammates. "The friendships that you have with other people, our fellow climbers, are terribly important to me," he emphasized. "When I get with Washburn or Bates or Houston, we start telling versions of the experiences we had years ago. Anybody who is as old as me has stories he likes to tell and every once in awhile, one of our children will say, 'Dad, that's story number twenty-three.' I hope I don't keep repeating the same story over and over, but I've got some wonderful memories."

John R. Durrance

Born:
July 20, 1912, Ocala, Florida
Hometown:
Denver, Colorado
Occupation:
Retired medical doctor
Climbing Highlights:
Rock climbs in Germany, New England and Wyoming. Mountain routes in the Alps, Tetons (including the first ascent, North Face of the Grand Teton), Sawtooths. Member of the 1939 American K2 expedition

"I'm surprised that mountaineering took the swing it did," said Jack Durrance. "When I was climbing in '36, there was hardly anybody the least bit interested in climbing and I probably wouldn't have been either if I hadn't been in Germany before that and climbed in Garmisch Park. In Munich, on the banks of the Isar, there were sandstone rocks. They called them *klettergartens*, climbing gardens. We used to go out and practice on those rocks just like they do here. It was something to do around the campsites, and we would find a boulder and pretend that we were 3,000 feet up, so it was a no-no to fall off. You had to climb it just as if you were up there that high and that was the name of the game. Now, kids that are bouldering often jump off of it. I'm surprised at how much they fall with a belay. Nothing is said about falling now, but boy, that was wrong in our day. If you were bouldering or climbing, you took particular pains not to fall, even though you might be just a few feet above the ground.

"In the Isar, the Schmit brothers [Franz and Toni], who first did the North Face of the Matterhorn, used to be there. Everybody would bicycle out and stand around and watch people do the routes. You had to grab a certain pebble by the proper hand or you didn't make it. These were very intricate, very difficult little pitches and these guys would climb as high as forty feet without a belay. They would work up to it very carefully, so rarely did anyone get hurt. It was good training.

"Then came the war, medicine, and a family and I was completely out of climbing and all of a sudden, everybody and his brother was into it in a big way. The techniques changed and they were doing aid climbing in Yosemite and climbing much harder routes. I must say that is so different than what we did. I sit back amazed. I read the *Alpine Journal* and what the guys have accomplished is hard to believe.

"I was in Germany for eight years from 1927 to 1935. I went to high school and was an apprentice in a factory, training to be a sales rep in America. That all washed out after Hitler took over Germany in 1933. I was there two years after the Nazis were in power. They had had enough of me and I had had enough of them, so I came back. High time, too. That wasn't very pleasant. I had had a smattering of climbing in Germany by then and I entered Dartmouth in 1935–36. That summer I went out to the Tetons and guided with [Paul] Petzoldt. The rock was magnificent. It was very reminiscent of the area on the Austrian-German border.

"However, I was very lazy. I did damn few climbs compared to what I could have done if there had been somebody around to climb with. I always led out there. I was always guiding and having fun, too. It was very casual. The only reason we did the north face of the Grand was that Weissner came in and when Petzoldt got wind of it he woke us up in the middle of the night and said, 'Let's get up there before he does.' I was not for it at all, because I don't like walls that have rocks falling on them all the time. That's not the proper place to be. But he wanted to do it so his brother and I went with him grudgingly. As soon as we got up the rock to where there was a little climbing, he said, 'Do you want to lead?' I smiled to myself. It wasn't a hard climb. There were a couple of pitches that were, but the falling rock really made me nervous."

Durrance and the Petzoldt brothers did traverse onto the North Ridge route prior to reaching the summit of the Grand Teton, but not before they had climbed the vast majority of the 3,000-foot route that later became one of the most famous in America.

Although he no longer climbs, Durrance travels and admires the mountains from a distance. "I went to Alaska two summers ago and saw Denali and, boy, have I got respect for the stupid people who go up on that. I would never have climbed that thing. Climbers today are crazy. They've got a death wish or something. Just the sheer labor of getting up Denali and facing that weather. If you climbed it in nice weather, it would be a nice walk. But they do it in blizzards with the wind blowing at how many miles an hour and at far below-zero weather. I'm not one of these dedicated do or die climbers. I like the challenge of a good rock climb. I've done very little ice climbing—some snow mixed with rock. On a good day and on solid ice or good rock on a ridge, it's fun. I'm not for being killed. I didn't always make the top or bull my way up in a storm because I didn't see the point in it. In climbing, if you respect the weather, which is your greatest danger, it's enjoyable and you come out. A lot of people in Europe go for weekends and they have an objective and they do a few daring things because if they don't make it, they've got to wait for another weekend before they can get back to it. That's too bad, because when things aren't right, you ought to turn around and go home. That's what I owe my longevity to.

"This is all subsequent to an experience I had when I was fifteen with another German teenager who was sixteen. We did a very difficult climb called Scharnit-spitze, and it was difficult in the German ratings. It was more difficult than I had ever tried. I have Osgood-Slaughters disease in my knees and I couldn't touch rock with them at that time. They were very tender. I've gotten better since then, although I've lost all the cartilage in my knees now. Osgood-Slaughters really handicapped me. Anyway, we climbed and climbed and we were ill-equipped. We had no clothing and it was late October. We had no watch. We had no matches. We had no food. We were just a couple of—they called us *gipfelstormers*, summit stormers, a favorite German word for anybody that runs up mountains. We got up on top of this thing and it got dark. You have to rappel off the top and my friend had been on top by a different route and he couldn't remember how to get down. We didn't have coats or anything. October, mind you. So we got off the summit and a little further down the ridge and piled a few loose stones up in a wall. They fell off on all sides. The clouds came in and it started to rain and it was a cold rain until midnight and then it started to snow. We didn't have any clothes so we kept our heads warm by putting the knapsacks over our heads. We kept our hands warm by putting them in each others shirts to keep them from freezing. It snowed from midnight until light. We began to freeze and my friend began to [experience the late stages of hypothermia] and didn't want to stir. I cried for help, which was foolish because there was no one around. We finally pissed on our hands and uncoiled a rope that was like steel because it was frozen. We made a couple of rappels and got down over the rocks and some of the snow was melting and we almost drowned in some of the places because the whole place was alive with runoff water, but we finally got back to camp. That was a miserable, miserable experience. They had the church bells ringing for us and my professor put on his climbing gear and went out with the guides until they found us asleep in the mountain hut. We had made tea and put our clothes up to dry. They gave us hell. They wrote us up in the Munich newspapers and it was a big deal. When I went to school the next day, I just sat there. My professor came in and said, 'Aren't you going to say good morning? You come back from the jaws of death and you won't even say good morning.' When that was all over, I swore that I'd never go ill-equipped again.

"I could afford to be well-equipped, because I always led so the guy behind me would have to carry it, so what the hell." Durrance laughed.

Like many climbers, Durrance was interested in skiing. He became involved in racing and, in 1935, entered the Olympic trials in the downhill. He came in second, but took a fall in one of the later races and ended up in bed for six weeks. He missed the last trial race and so did not qualify, but his brother did ski in the 1936 Olympics. Durrance made a comeback and, in 1938, he was the Eastern Downhill Champion.

"I got some notoriety by skiing down the headwall at Tuckerman's Ravine," he said, "but I nearly killed myself. I would go down slopes that others thought a little foolish."

The pace of climbing has changed drastically in recent years, according to Durrance. "Back in the fifties, you could read everything that was written about new climbs and keep up with it. Now, I don't think anyone can keep up. There's so much being written. Everybody climbs and they do horribly difficult things. They don't seem to give a damn.

"After the war, and I'm speaking of World War I, the Germans had lost the war and their youth had absolutely nothing to be proud of, nothing to look forward to—they were lost kids. The only way that they could prove their manhood was to climb mountains, and they started an upswing in mountaineering like we've had in the States since World War II. They did a lot of climbing in the Alps and a few got over to the Himalayas, but these were rare compared to the plethora of climbs that take place now. At that time, they had the attitude that they had to prove themselves, and if they got killed in the process, it was national pride that they were upholding. I don't think that the Americans are upholding any national pride, but they're upholding—I don't know what motivates them. I think the threat of the atom bomb has something to do with it. I don't know what motivates some guys to go up, for instance, the East Face of Everest. Not only do they climb very difficult routes, but they've got all these objective dangers, avalanches, that they face and they walk into that with their eyes open and their chances are—well, you take all the expeditions and see how many people are lost and you'll find that the chances are not too good of coming back from one of those big peaks. What motivates this generation after World War II to do this? I think it's a kickback from the war and what they have to face. Just as the Germans. It's easy to understand. They had lost the war, all their honor, they had nothing to look forward to, and they were trying to prove something by difficult climbs.

"Today, young people look around at the world and they say, 'Why not do it? That damn thing will explode someday and we'll be killed anyway.' That might be the philosophy that lies behind the unnecessary risk they take.

"If you are exploring on a ship, going to a new world, it has some purpose. If you are trying to shinny up a rock or snow slope, it doesn't. That's why I talk about the futility of the future. Atom bombs scare the hell out of me, too. The potentials are there. Somebody just has to send them and the world is gone. There will be a few that live somewhere, and they will repopulate the place, but that's a grim future. Some people commit suicide. For others, it's just short of committing suicide when they go to a place where they have less of a chance of coming back than they have of dying. Maybe that's what pushes them."

Many a climber today would give anything to have had one situation that Durrance experienced. "I had the Tetons all to myself, like Adam and Eve in the Garden," he laughed. "I'd hate to have to stand in line to do a climb. That's one of the reasons to go to the Himalayas now. It isn't that crowded, although the routes on Everest are getting so they have to space you. If I were climbing now and really in shape, and I went off to the Baltoro Glacier and the Trango Towers and got lost in some of that area, that would be fine. I'm sure that the time will come when you will go into even that area and see somebody else everyday.

"I've enjoyed all my climbing. I remember we were walking up the trail [in the Tetons] and we said, 'Let's do the North Face of Nez Perce, the hourglass. It looks like fun.' So we pile up there and we do a first ascent and that was the way it was. You would be nursing a hangover and say, 'Well let's do this or that,' and it could be a first.

"The thing that interested me as much as anything was route finding. To look at a face that seemed impossible, when you knew that was not true. We always found a way up because none of it was that hard. It wasn't like Yosemite, where you had to be precise so you would know where to pendulum or something. We just picked out a ridge and said, 'Let's do that one today.'

"I liked the relaxed attitude we had then. What I hate is the 'do or die' attitude. Everybody wants to rack up a first ascent for himself and I wasn't opposed to that. I like to have virgin territory. You can hardly find that anymore, but I don't think it has to be pushed so hard. And it's not the youth. It's the guys in their twenties and thirties who are doing the really hard stuff.

"I'm sure that everybody gets a physical satisfaction out of deprivation and hardships, and then winning and getting a nice warm bed. Who hasn't sat in a bivouac or been benighted, that hasn't dreamed of a nice soft bed and maybe something in that bed? Then, having weathered it out and having experienced the contrast of roughing it and the softness of civilization, one appreciates the softness.

"I enjoyed the challenge. I enjoyed my ability to be on my own. Everybody likes that feeling of doing it by yourself. You are responsible for accomplishing it. It's a proving ground for your ability to survive under difficult conditions. People like to get away from our soft civilization and be rugged. The Peace Corps is motivated somewhat the same way. They don't do dangerous and daring things, but they do uncomfortable things. They do like our forefathers did. They relive that, and they get the feel of something that is a little more difficult. People feel that civilization is pretty soft. You really don't have to do much except sit around and have people bring you food, and die of heart failure.

"What is there left to do that would impress the rest of the climbers? I think everybody's out to impress their fellow man. They're trying to say, 'Look at me, I'm alive and look at what I have done.' You've got to do a hell of a lot now to impress anyone. Nothing in mountaineering really impresses anyone anymore. They push it just about to the limit."

Arlene Blum

Born:
March 1, 1945, Davenport, Iowa
Hometown:
Berkeley, California
Occupation:
Writer, lecturer
Climbing Highlights:

McKinley, Annapurna (leader of first American ascent), Everest (1976 American Bicentennial expedition), Noshaq (Afghanistan), Bringupanth (first ascent), and peaks in Peru, Tanzania, and Kashmir (three first ascents). Also a six-week trek across the Alps, and a ten-month trek across the Himalayas

For every expedition that goes to climb a mountain, someone must plan and organize. Arlene Blum has, more often than not, found herself with that responsibility.

"I like organizing things," she said. "I get a great deal of satisfaction from having a dream and then making it happen."

Blum, who holds a Ph.D. in biophysical chemistry, began climbing in a physical education class at Reed College in Portland, Oregon. After she had climbed extensively in the northwest, she ran into a problem.

"I had done a number of expeditions with my friends from Reed. But when I first applied to go on Himalayan expeditions, women just weren't invited. So finally I decided to try to organize my own. I have also organized mixed expeditions, but the all-women ones are the best known."

This skill carried beyond her climbing to science and community events. Each year she helps organize an event that combines her interests in planning and the high mountains.

"I organize a big Himalayan fair in Berkeley which is really satisfying. We have arts and crafts, entertainment, food, Himalayan people, and lots of fun. I was amazed, after I dreamed it up, that 6,000 people came the first year and have continued to attend each year since.

In fact, it may have been the combination of skills that attracted Blum to climbing in the first place.

"It's an ultimate challenge. You get to use all of your skills—physical, mental, and spiritual and focus on one goal. When you reach the summit, you know you're there. It's a very discreet, defined goal, unlike most activities in life where, after you reach one summit, there's always more to do.

"Now that I have a young child, I don't want to do anything that is life-threatening. I enjoy trips like the Bringupanth expedition, which was a first ascent of a 22,000-foot peak and relatively free of objective danger. I prefer exploration to climbing high peaks. Twenty-thousand-foot peaks are fine.

"There are lots of unclimbed peaks in areas that are still restricted, so westerners can't go. They will open up eventually. I have friends over there who might tell me where, so I can get a permit when they open."

She paused in thought, then continued, "Having a child can be an adventure. It doesn't have to be climbing mountains. I do like to dream something up and make it happen."

The aspect of climbing that Blum finds most interesting is probing the unknown.

"I like exploration. I like doing first ascents. I'm not a great technical climber, but I enjoy going to an area that has not been visited, or is hardly explored, and picking out routes and climbing unclimbed peaks.

"I spent ten months walking 2,200 miles up and down and across the Himalayas. We figured on the altimeter that we averaged about 3,000 feet elevation change a day for ten months. You would go from a river at 1,000 feet up to a pass at 19,000 feet, down to a river at 2,000 and over a pass at 15,000. Good exercise!"

Through her work on a book detailing the history of women in mountaineering, Blum has had the chance to talk with many people about climbing.

"People like Lynn Hill use a whole new vocabulary associated with the rock climbing competitions. You can't do first ascents so easily any more and people are turning to sport climbing as opposed to adventure climbing. The potential for really new adventure is diminished. Areas that are restricted politically are where there are still adventures left, with new routes and exploration.

In *Annapurna: A Women's Place*, her book about the all-woman ascent, Blum wrote, "The greatest rewards come only from the greatest commitment."

"I believe that," she said. "I think that one of the lessons of climbing is perseverance, having a vision and continuing on in spite of obstacles, putting one foot in front of another steadily until you get to your goal. Learning that lesson in mountaineering helps you apply it to all other activities."

But Blum has also seen how quickly a small mistake can lead to tragedy in mountaineering. On the Annapurna climb, the two members of the second summit team, Alison Chadwick-Onyszkiewicz and Vera Watson, fell to their deaths on the descent.

Blum wrote, "I sat numbly in the snow, unaware of what was happening around me as disconnected images of Vera and Alison ran through my mind. I thought of Vera in her sunny kitchen, preparing a wonderful meal for us, or dancing up a rock face, every move made with style and grace. And Alison—I saw her at Noshaq base camp arm in arm with Janusz, or playing with the children on the trail to Annapurna."

She said, "I think people that have experiences that are on the edge of life and death want to tell people about them and people want to read about them. Climbing is a real ultimate activity."

Jack Tackle
Born:
September 17, 1953, San Jose, California
Hometown:
Bozeman, Montana
Occupation:
Sporting goods sales representative,
professional mountain guide
Climbing Highlights:
Mt. Siguniang (China), Everest (to 27,000 feet), Lukpilla
Brakk (Pakistan, first ascent), Mt. Hunter, Diamond Arete (first
ascent), Mt. Waddington, (third ascent overall, new route), Mt.
McKinley, Isis Face (first ascent). New routes in the Cordillera
Huayhuash of Peru, the Kichatna Spires, Juneau Ice Fields, and
Coastal Range of Alaska, and in the region of Mt. Kennedy in
the Yukon

It's not an easy way to make a living and sometimes it's outright dangerous, but guiding clients on the classic mountain routes has paid the bills for many climbers. Among the best guides in the country, Jack Tackle knows what the business is about.

He held up his hand, the fingers engulfed in a balloon of white bandages. Tackle had been guiding when a client dislodged a rock, which landed on the fourth finger of his right hand, cutting off the tip. He taped the tip back on, put his hand in a glove and splinted the injured finger with tape to the two fingers on either side of it. Several hours later, a doctor sewed the tip back on.

"Guiding and climbing are mutually exclusive," he remarked. "I've never been hurt climbing, but when you are guiding, there's always a chance that the client will make a mistake."

He recalled an accident where guide Kim Schmitz had been leading a difficult route when a rope snagged. He fell backwards off the cliff, landing some eighty feet below on a narrow ledge between two sets of jagged rocks.

"The allure of being a guide wore off the day Schmitz hit the ledge," Tackle said. "Guides have a saying that clients exist for three reasons—to try to kill other clients, to try to kill themselves and, most importantly, to try to kill you.

"Schmitz's client pulled him off. When he hit the ledge, his feet exploded. He's had sixteen operations on them. He'll never be the same. It's a little scary in the sense that so much of our lives is focused towards the physical. It's like any professional athlete. A halfback in the NFL gets his knees blown up and what does he do? Your physical capabilities are tied to what you do. I have other things to fall back on, but I'd be lying if I said I wouldn't have a hard time filling the void if climbing was taken away from me. It's something that is not just a passing interest."

"Climbing is relatively safe, more so than the public perception of it. Part of the challenge of climbing is the mental position it puts you in to make judgments and decisions that not only determine your own safety, but other people's safety. You're exercising your mental capabilities at a high level of stress for fairly high stakes, and when you make the right judgments and you do the right things, that is really satisfying."

While growing up, Tackle was involved in several organized sports in high school and college. When those were finished, he felt something was missing. Then a friend took him rock climbing. Although he didn't know anything about climbing and admitted, "I think I had heard of Hillary and Everest," he knew instantly that he liked the sport.

"It seemed to come naturally to me. I started in Montana, so my interest developed into alpine climbing and mountaineering instead of starting with warm weather rock climbing like most people probably do.

"The reason I was attracted to climbing initially was for the physical movement of it, like other athletes who like their particular motions. There is something ridiculously nice about cramponing. Then it became more than the motion because the mountains are the only venue, the only place, where I feel totally at home. I don't have to be climbing necessarily, but to be involved in the stimulation of the mountain environment, well, there is nothing else that comes close to matching it. I've chosen to live and do certain things in my life that are not nearly as stressful at times, but still, I feel a need to be in the mountains and be climbing to keep my brains from turning to mush."

Two routes have been particularly important to Tackle. The first was a 1977 climb made with Ken Currens on the south face of Mt. Waddington, the highest peak in British Columbia. "That climb was interesting because we did a new route and it was the first time the face had been climbed since 1942, when Fred Beckey and his brother climbed it. Also, the first ascent was done by [Fritz] Weissner in '36, so it's special because both Weissner and Beckey told me it was one of their two or three best climbs, and both of them launched into the forefront of American climbing after they went to Waddington. Weissner went to K2 and almost got up it without oxygen [in 1939]. On the way back from Waddington, he did the second ascent of the north ridge of the Grand Teton and the [first mountaineering] ascent of Devils Tower. Beckey was nineteen when he did Waddington and that pushed him right into the middle of things for the next thirty or forty years."

The other important climb was a new route on McKinley in 1982, called the Isis Face. Tackle climbed the 8,000-foot face with Dave Stutzman, who died later that year in an avalanche while working as a ski patrolman. The route was the hardest climb on Mt. McKinley at the time.

Tackle, who has been on more than fifteen expeditions, got a big break when another climber dropped out of the 1983 American Everest West Ridge expedition. Tackle was invited to fill the spot on a team that included John Roskelley and Galen Rowell.

"There were no assumptions that I would be one of the lead climbers. I thought I would be somewhere in the middle," Tackle noted. "It just happens that I was lucky and stayed healthy and got to be out front a lot of the time. I started realizing that there might be a chance I could get up it. I hadn't put any pressure on myself, and I didn't have any pressure from outside like Roskelley, Rowell, and Schmitz had. They were expected to perform a lot more than I was, because of ties to companies they work for and also to the climbing world. Those guys have reputations. They are higher profile than me, so I didn't have as much pressure and I think it was a benefit."

When other climbers retreated from the mountain for various reasons, Tackle found himself at 25,000 feet, where he stayed for ten nights without oxygen. He eventually made it to 27,000 feet, the team's high point, before a storm brought the expedition to a close.

"When you're sitting up there at Camp V, trying to get to the summit of Everest, you know that if you get there, things are probably going to be a little bit easier for you in your job, although the meaning of that, the importance of that, has changed because so many people have climbed Everest. It still means more than if you haven't climbed it, but it doesn't have that Hillary, Unsoeld, Hornbein, Whittaker, phenomenon that happened in the past.

"The way I am trying to make a living has to do with being a little more high profile than the average, not just because of guiding, but because of sales repping and the advertising, pictures, and articles that are associated with the type of trips I am doing now. The guys who are really good at this are older. Galen is fourteen years older than I am. It all goes hand in hand. If you want to do successful expeditions, you need good funding. You need good organization. You need good contacts, and if you're Joe Schmuck and they've never heard of you, it's hard. The more well-known you are, the easier it is to get things organized and funded. Success breeds success. Certain people go for that part of it more than others. I would rather be like the guys I have tended to climb with and let the actions speak for themselves, but you have to do a little bit of self-promotion. You can't just stand around and wait for it to fall on you. If you are trying to make a living out of it, you've got to go out and push a little bit."

Tackle had a chance to return to Everest, but he turned down the offer because of his job. Six members of that team made the summit, including one who had been with him in 1983. "Persistence counts. You go back [to Everest] if you have any concern for the long term."

The drive to climb the highest mountain in the world has infected countless climbers in history. The less than ideal climbing conditions on the mountain and the long wait, often years, for permits have stopped some climbers, but still, it is Everest. Tackle tried to explain Everest's lure. "If you get close or do well—it's a hard thing to describe—but there is a trap you fall into with Everest."

His ten-day stay at 25,000 feet left him "hammered" following the expedition, and the next year he returned from Lukpilla Brakk in Pakistan with malaria and dysentery.

"Expeditions tend to disrupt your personal life, your financial life and your health. The more you go on expeditions, the more chance there is of repeating all those things. I've been through all of them a couple of times, so I tend to be pretty open-eyed about what the effects of expeditions are. Expedition climbing versus climbing in the States is really different. It's a whole different aspect.

"Even though the trip to Pakistan was successful and we didn't have to spend a lot of time or money, I'm probably going to go to Alaska more and do routes up there. It's cheap. You don't have to change your money. You can't get malaria. You don't have to deal with L.O.'s [liason officers] or ministers of tourism, and it's real climbing. There are unclimbed things in the Kichatnas, in the Alaska Range, in the St. Elias Range. I'd like to do new routes on the other major peaks near McKinley. The routes that are left are usually either real hard or real dangerous, but it's amazing that there are some left that are reasonable in both categories."

William A. "Al" Read

Born:

November 19, 1936, Washington, D.C.

Hometown:

San Francisco, California

Occupation:

Owner, adventure travel business, and climbing guide

Climbing Highlights:

1969 American Dhaulagiri Expedition (deputy leader), Nepal-American Gauri Shankar Expedition (leader, first ascent). Lived in Kathmandu five years organizing and setting up numerous expeditions to the Himalayas. Mt. McKinley (first ascent of East Buttress), and peaks in Colorado, Wyoming, and California

High altitude mountaineers dread pulmonary edema. This building of fluid in the lungs, caused by the stress of hard work at high altitudes, usually means terrible sickness and the potential end of an expedition. Sometimes it means death. But for Al Read, ironically, a case of pulmonary edema may have saved his life.

Read was deputy leader of a 1969 American expedition to the Himalayas. Theirs would be the first expedition into the region after a five-year ban on all climbing in Nepal. In the spring of 1962, Woodrow Wilson Sayre, a Tufts University professor and grandson of the president, and his three companions had a permit to climb Gyachung Kang near the Nepal-China border.

Read recalled the controversy surrounding the expedition. "Sayre went over a pass and went down on the Chinese side, the Tibetan side, and onto the Rongbuk Glacier and tried to climb Everest. He failed and came back and told everybody about it. China was upset and Nepal wanted to maintain relations with China. It was a time of chaos there with the Dalai Lama having recently fled to India. Khampas were active in Tibet, so Nepal closed its peaks to climbing in 1964."

By 1969, Nepal had lifted the ban and Read and some friends sent in a long list of peaks for which they wanted permits. The Nepalese government responded with a permit for Dhaulagiri.

"We decided to do a different route than had been done before. We made our approach and one day I went from 7,000 feet to 15,000 feet and developed cerebral and pulmonary edema. It really surprised me because I had been on McKinley and had been okay, but this time I went too high too fast.

"I was in a coma and was evacuated by Jim Morrissey, who played in a lot of events later in the Himalayas. The coma lasted for thirty-six hours and I woke up blind in one eye from retinal hemorrhages."

Morrissey reported that Read's pulse was 160 and his breathing was sixty respirations per minute so Read's next move was downward. Meanwhile, the rest of the expedition moved upward.

A team of eight climbers was working on the East Dhaulagiri Glacier. They had been hauling loads and were ready to place several logs over a crevasse, when they heard a roar. They quickly sought cover on the mountain and an avalanche swept down over the top of them.

"It wasn't just a snow avalanche, it was an ice avalanche," Read explained. "The only one who wasn't killed was Lou Reichardt."

Reichardt, who had managed to find only a small indentation in the slope for protection, stood up after the avalanche, hoping to see his teammates. No one was in sight. He tried to probe for bodies, but the ice blocks made such work useless and he was forced to make a lonely walk back to base camp. He later called the aftermath of the avalanche "a scene of indescribable violence, reminiscent of the first eons of creation."

"Reichardt was the only one who was spared," said Read. "And he went back with the 1973 American Dhaulagiri Expedition and climbed to the summit."

Thinking about his close call with death, Read said, "I could have been one of the seven. The only thing that saved me was that I had pulmonary edema. I was very distressed that all these people had been killed. The whole scene, the remote location, the circumstances that everyone was in, made it a heavy-duty adventure. Nepal is not so remote now, but that part of Nepal really was then."

But Read wasn't ready to quit climbing. He remembered another dangerous time. "When I was sixteen, I climbed the North Face of the Grand Teton with a friend. We had to bivouac because we got off route. There was some rockfall and snow and rain, and on the summit he said he would never climb again. He hung up his equipment after that. I've never thought of giving up."

But he has changed in one sense. "Because I had pulmonary edema that time and don't acclimatize well, I am always hesitant to climb too high because, one, I don't want to die and, two, I don't want to screw up everybody else by making them drag me back down."

Read worked for several years in Nepal helping expeditions secure porters, Sherpas, and other necessary arrangements. To do this, he had to work closely with the Nepalese officials.

"Because of my position in Nepal and because we had very good relations with the mountaineering powers that be, I could have engineered a permit for any peak at any time while I was there. If I hadn't had this potential acclimatization problem, I would have been on a big expedition at least once every year and I'd probably be an extremely successful Himalayan climber, or I'd be dead."

These connections did come into play when Nepal opened several unclimbed peaks to joint expeditions. "One of them was a real prize peak called Gauri Shankar. It's not real high, it's 24,400 feet, but it's a very significant landmark peak and a very hard peak. Probably because of the connections I had then, I was able to persevere over a stack of applications from Europe and Japan. I had to negotiate to establish who the team would be and I put together a team that was half Nepali and half American. John Roskelley and Dorji (a Sherpa) reached the summit and it was a very proud day because it was the first ascent of a difficult route. In fact, the mountain was tried every year for several years and was not climbed again until 1984.

"It was a 9,000-foot face with steep ice, rock, and direct aid climbing very far from anywhere. The Sherpas were doing a very high standard of climbing and really were hanging in there."

While Read was working in Nepal, he became involved in an unusual paper battle. The Nepalese government had approved an application for a commercial promotional activity that Read disagreed with. His objection prevailed and, as he said, "I stopped a company from landing a helicopter on top of Everest. I'm proud of that."

Read's father was a geologist, so he spent much of his youth outdoors on field trips. His parents gave him a book called *High Conquest* by James Ramsey Ullman. "In it were some classic tales of early climbing, Himalayan expeditions mainly, and I became fascinated with it, really fascinated with it. I read about Mallory and Irvine disappearing on the north side of Everest in 1924, and stories involving the Eiger." When he moved to Colorado, he took a class with the Colorado Mountain Club. He climbed around the western United States and made the twenty-fifth ascent of Devils Tower and the fourteenth ascent of Shiprock. "These weren't first ascents," he said, "but it was early enough that people were still counting."

"From my deepest and oldest memories, I was always fascinated with the mountains. They had a magical quality about them and climbing was part of that. What caused that, I don't know. It was as if, though it's sort of foolish, I was reincarnated from some other mountain climber.

"In climbing, you can have a very intense, sometimes spiritual, highly emotional adventure and you can turn around and have another one. That kind of thing keeps a lot of people doing it. They can't find the same experience doing something else. It is certainly satisfying achieving something in the business world or in art—and climbing is more of an art than it is a sport.

"It's an adventure, and adventure is very hard to find in the modern world. Going to the moon is no doubt an adventure, but traditional adventure is real hard to find. There are no more uncharted seas. What is adventure? It's an area that's hazardous. In order to have an adventure, you have to have an element of danger. That's part of the definition. The threat of bodily injury puts a little bit of daring into it. In the mountains you are working with both your body and your mind. A lot of people think climbing is a physical thing, but you have to concentrate on what you are doing. It's goal-oriented in the sense that the goal is trying to get to the top. It's action and reward. You are doing something and you get gratification when you reach the top. The whole experience on a serious climb is very intense because the danger factor is there.

"The forces of nature are astonishing, and it's so beautiful up there that it is unbelievable. Once on Mt. McKinley, I stopped at 19,000 feet going over a pass. A storm was coming and I looked around and thought, 'I'm going to do this for the rest of my life.'"

Christian Bonington

Born:
August 6, 1934, London, England
Hometown:
Wigton, Cumbria, England
Occupation:
Writer, lecturer, photographer
Climbing Highlights:
Annapurna II (first ascent, 1960), Nuptse (first ascent, 1961),
Central Pillar of Freney (first ascent, 1961), North Wall of The
Eiger (first British ascent, 1962), Central Tower of Paine (first
ascent, 1962), Brammah (first ascent, 1973), Changabang (first
ascent, 1974), Ogre (first ascent, 1977), Kongur (1981), Vinson
(1984), and Everest (1985)

The British have a long tradition of climbing exploration in the Himalayas.
Much of that tradition is based on the work of Chris Bonington, recipient of the
Founder's Medal of the Royal Geographical Society, and a veteran leader with
more than fifteen consecutive yearly visits to the highest mountains in the world.

"I look at climbing not so much as standing on top as seeing the other side,"
Bonington explained. "There are always other horizons in front of you, other
horizons to go beyond and that's what I like about climbing.

"Climbing is a series of explorations and discoveries. It is full of excitement
and the unknown. Actually, I think for most people, their most exciting climbing
is done in their first two years, when they are learning the most about their own
limits."

Bonington was raised in London. On a vacation, he was traveling through
Wales and "saw someone climbing on a rock and I knew instinctively that climbing
was something I wanted to do."

His climbing career very nearly came to a quick end when he took a nine-to-
five job with a British corporation, thinking that his three-week vacation each year
would be enough for the amount of climbing he wanted to do. He felt stifled in
the job and soon learned that he wanted to climb more than anything else and
started looking for a way to climb and still make a living.

He took up photojournalism and received what he called "adventure theme
assignments." One such assignment sent him to Baffin Island to photograph Eskimos. Bonington recalled, "The temperature was minus forty and it was totally
quiet and beautiful. I went out for two weeks with some Eskimos, hunting caribou.
We didn't see any caribou, but we did see some impressive country."

A later assignment took him to Ethiopia on a descent of the Blue Nile. He nearly drowned when his boat overturned, but that was only the beginning. "We were attacked by local natives. We were ambushed and got away. Then they attacked at night. That was the only time I ever fired shots in anger. I don't think I hit anything, but I fired five shots. Then I decided I'd had enough of this photojournalism bit. I was tired of being a voyeur, sitting back while others did things, so I decided to get something of my own going."

That led him to the Alps where, among other things, he accomplished the first British ascent of the Eiger North Face, an event that placed him in the headlines. He was asked to write a book and give a few lectures and he hasn't stopped doing either for over twenty-five years. His books include *I Chose to Climb, The Next Horizon, Kongur: China's Elusive Summit, Everest: The Unclimbed Ridge, Annapurna South Face, Everest South West Face, The Quest for Adventure, Everest The Hard Way,* and *The Everest Years.* Literally thousands of climbing enthusiasts have heard his lectures and viewed his slide presentations over the years.

In *The Next Horizon,* Bonington wrote:

One of the features of climbing is the intensity of concentration it exacts. In its basic form, if you are poised on a rock wall a hundred feet above the ground, all other thoughts and problems are engulfed by the need for absolute concentration. There is no room for anything other than the problems of staying in contact with the rock and negotiating the next few moves. In this respect, climbing offers an escape, or perhaps it would be better to describe it as a relaxation, from everyday worries of human relationships, money, or jobs. This relaxation lasts for longer than just those moments when you are actually climbing and life is in jeopardy.

Sitting on a ledge, belaying one's partner, senses are extra acute; the feel of the rock under hand, of the wind and sun, the shape of the hills—all these are perceived with an extra intensity. Absorption in immediate surroundings once again excludes one's everyday life. On an expedition the same withdrawal from everyday affairs takes place, but here the expedition becomes a tiny little world of its own with, in microcosm, between its members, all the tensions and conflict that can take place in the larger world. The all-consuming aim is to climb the mountain of one's choice and this transcends, in importance, anything that might be happening beyond it.

One of the attractions, indeed reasons, for climbing is the element of risk involved, of pitting one's own judgment against the mountain, with a fall as the price of a mistake. In its purest sense, the solo climber is getting the most out of the sport since he is staking his life on his judgment. Without companions or rope, he has a good chance of being killed in a fall. The majority of us, however, prefer to hedge our bets, climbing with a companion, using a rope, and then contriving running belays to reduce the distance we fall if we do come off. The problem is in deciding just how far we should reduce this risk before losing a vital element in the sport.

He is still aware, however, that the sport he has chosen does exact a price. He has seen friends die in the mountains—Peter Boardman and Joe Tasker,

Ian Clough, Nick Estcourt, Mick Burke, Dougal Haston, and others. "It is like playing Russian roulette," he admitted. "You are exposed to a great many objective dangers for such a long time. If you do it year after year, the odds kind of pile up against you."

Bonington is able to look beyond those names in relationship to his own climbing. "I don't think about the accidents and the possibility of dying on a climb. I think you'd probably give up if you did that. I am an optimist. I blank that out. I'm worried, yes, but basically for my family. I get worried because of the responsibility to my family.

"I go climbing because I like climbing and I modify my climbing to what I enjoy. I'm now tending to go for the unclimbed peaks in the range of 23,000, 24,000, or 25,000 feet high that I can climb with enjoyment. The need to climb comes from inside. Basically, I enjoy stretching myself to my personal limits, and that's what the satisfaction is for me."

Bonington summed up his feelings by saying, "The allure is so great. I must go on. I don't think I could live without climbing."

T. I. M. Lewis

Born:
April 5, 1944, Aberyswyth, Wales

Died:
August 23, 1984, Sheffield, England

Occupation:
Editor

Climbing Highlights:
Rock climbs in the Lake District, Derbyshire, Scotland and Wales, routes in the Dolomites, Chamonix, and throughout the Alps, as well as Czechoslovakia, the United States, and Corsica. Several major spelunking expeditions

Tim Lewis sat down in the overstuffed chair in the Sheffield office of *Mountain* magazine. Boxes of papers covered a nearby table and avalanched off onto the floor surrounding the chair.

"We just delivered an issue of the magazine to the printer," he explained. "It gets so hectic around here the last few days before an issue is due. It's great to finish it, kind of like the feeling of being at the top of a really fine climb."

Lewis became editor of *Mountain* in 1978. Under his leadership the magazine grew steadily, eventually becoming international in scope.

"Writing is inherent in the sport," he explained. "It comes in two ways. You can be cynical and say it comes from the early days of Whimper and the idea that a good book, well illustrated, will sell well and provide money for more climbing trips. That's a long-running tradition in climbing and travel books in general. The other sort of literature is memoirs of people who are more exclusively national. They don't climb much outside the country, but they developed an area like the Lake District or Wales.

"How do you tell somebody else about a climb? You either tell them verbally or you write it down. You tell them, if you are altruistic, so they can go do this pleasurable thing for themselves and avoid the unnecessary pitfalls of going the wrong way, or you write it to say what a good bloke you are."

Lewis began climbing in school because "you had a choice. You either joined the cadet force and wore a uniform for some part of the army or navy or air force, or you were a Boy Scout. I started off in the cadet force and it became clear that I wasn't really suited for the military life and so I was brushed off on the Scouts. I wasn't too unhappy about that because a couple of my mates were in the Scouts. We used to have one field day every term and the cadet force used to play soldier around the school ground, but the Scouts used to get to go away somewhere, which was a better deal. I was about fifteen or sixteen and we went to Harrison's Rocks, the classic London crags. It was safe for kids because you top-rope everything anyway. You've got a lad at one end of the rope and a lad at the other end of the rope and it's tied to a tree, so not a lot of grief can come of that. So we took to going down there on our own in the evenings as well.

"Most of my experience in climbing has been in the classic British tradition, really. I started rock climbing in England and Scotland and Wales, and then went to the Alps, which were the next immediate big range. When I started climbing in the sixties, that was what you did. It was even sort of more specified how you did it. I mean the traditional English trip was to go first to the Dolomites because there the climbing was rock climbing, which we had done at home and we were good at, better than them," he laughed. "Therefore, even though they were big, you could do the rock climbs, which got you fit on 2,000-foot routes in the Dolomites. Then on the way back, because that's on the far end of the Alps, you passed through Chamonix, as a rule, and with this newfound fitness you had a do-about with some of the routes there. That wasn't a binding obligation, but it was certainly one of the tendencies. The conditions in the Dolomites are better earlier in the year. University terms tend to end in June or early July and that's a touch early for Chamonix. So that's what I did. Then as [my interests and abilities] developed over the years, I went to climbing in North America in many of the rock areas there.

"I enjoy the act of being climbing. When you drive out of the city of Sheffield, you cross from the county of Yorkshire into the county of Derbyshire. The city stops pretty quickly. You come to this ridgeline and in front of you is countryside. Behind you is town. When you are there, whether it's for the afternoon or for the evening, you are a climber. That's your purpose and it all seems to make sense when you are doing it, and it seems to make sense of the rest of your life because it's summed up. I remember MacIntosh's famous phrase describing a Himalayan desperate he had just done. He said that after doing a route like that, he could stand living in Huddersfield for six months. I suppose you could say Philadelphia, or Pittsburgh, or someplace else in America as well.

"I enjoy the physical exercise, the fact that it is outdoors, the fact that in a way it is anarchic. You can do it on your own, you set your own rules. These are all very simple objectives and they are very satisfying to the mind. The trouble is that you grow older, along with the rest of the world, and what you have to do impinges upon the time you have to get that simplicity.

"And I don't think climbing is all that dangerous. You set your own risk. I've read these psychological articles that say climbers don't get along with their fathers and have a death wish. I always felt this was wrong. Most of the climbers I know have no death wish at all. They have an enormous life wish. The risk was life. All life's a risk. It's a bloody lie—people thinking they can live a safe life. There is no such thing as a safe life. You set your own risk all the time, every day. It does vary for each person, because I don't think there are any common denominators to climbers at all. It lies in that vicarious area, not in any molded area, any childhood unhappiness, or anything else. When you start to talk academically about climbing, the contrast between the expressions and the reality of what you know about climbing are great.

"That's the area in which climbing becomes an art, because it allows for individual expression. Two people can climb an identical piece of rock, one well and one badly. One can make it look like ballet and the other can make it look like a team of elephants at random. In another level of personality, it is possible to see in such classic things as Herman Buhl's solo ascent of Nanga Parbat, an immense element of the man's style. That's easy to see. You could also see it in the activities of people who climb rock. John Gill's personality in terms of bouldering. In Britain, we have the Joe Brown route, the classic line. You could allegedly park Brown at the foot of a completely blank piece of rock, about which nobody knew anything, and he'd pick the plumb line. Maybe not on the first time, but he'd climb three routes and they'd all be good. And you could park some other duffer there and he'd climb the meat and three veg. and ignore the good rock because of personality, intelligence and, when it's all said and done, some unique matter in Brown that draws him to this sort of rock and sends all other mortals scuttling for cover in what looks like an easier way up the crag."

When Lewis was at the top of his form, he looked at other climbers and noticed a difference between them and the way he felt inside. "There was a period when I was about twenty-five when I was one of the better climbers in the country, but I knew that I wasn't going to be Joe Brown. I could see in other people some kind of spark that I didn't have. Some of them have like a rat gnawing at their bowels which makes them climb, climb all the time. Others had a more cold-bloodedly calculated approach or a sense of bravado. It's never been the only thing I've done. In fact, for quite long periods of each year, I don't climb. Usually in the winter. In my youth, I always played rugby in the winter and climbed in the summer. I suppose I get a relief from it in that way. I certainly find, after a certain amount of climbing, you get burned out on it. I'm not sure if it's weeks or months on rock climbing, or moments on something horrendous and huge." He laughed. "Your interest wanes very appreciably when confronted with this 10,000-foot avalanching face, the middle of which you are supposed to be doing. You lose interest in the flash of an eye.

"I know that the accusation was always leveled against me by people who had climbed with me when I climbed very hard and well that I always did it for amusement only, that I didn't like it when I had to stop laughing. I never have liked it when I stopped laughing. I always felt that to be a good climber you must be able to do it laughing, smiling, cigarette in the corner of the mouth. It should be casual. It shouldn't be such a balls-out effort all the time.

"Mountaineering creates an interest in a deeper sense. It has a haunting charisma, that blackness, that risk that you are playing with. It is of interest to people. It *must* be of interest to people—how many *Omens* have they made, how many *Poltergeists*? How many other horror movies have they made that take you to the edge and confront you with things you didn't think you could stand and then bring you back again? That's what climbing is about, as well.

"When you go climbing, you're on your own. It's rare to be under close scrutiny even on a popular rock. Climbing produces a situation where the mind reacts in a way which is otherwise only achieved by mystics or by conscious meditation or by very unfortunate and much more brutal stress. You take somebody at the top of a huge Himalayan mountain and it's small wonder that he begins to think he's got a friend with him. He's deranged through physical and mental processes which are quite incomprehensible. For people who have had religious experiences, or who have been in concentration camps or something like that, the world finds it absolutely understandable that you should see God when a man points a gun at you. It's equally understandable that you should see God when you are bloody well near Him standing on top of a mountain."

Timothy Ifor Morgan Lewis died of an extended illness one year after this interview. His associate at Mountain *magazine, Paul Nunn, read an address at the Sheffield Crematorium that ended with this tribute: "In primitive human belief only kings, poets, chieftains, and magicians were privileged to be reborn. Countless less distinguished souls wandered disconsolately in the icy grounds of the Castle, uncheered by modern Christian hopes of resurrection. Tim was both spiritual and a secularist, but his presence could be uplifting, his person mercurial, and where can he have gone but to Caer Arianrhod, the place beyond the North West Wind, if not into the blaze of the sun itself. The Celtic Heaven."*

César Morales Arnao

Born:
November 28, 1923, Huaraz, Peru

Hometown:
Lima, Peru

Occupation:
Journalist, Peruvian Minister
of Mountaineering

Climbing Highlights:

Numerous climbs in the Andes Mountains of Peru including Cupa
Sur, Ishinca, Vallunaraju, Hualcan Oeste, Pisco, Rimarinma, Urus
Central, Yanapakca Oeste, Huandoy, Aguja Nevada Oeste, and
other peaks in the Cordilleras Huayhuash, Raura, Vilcabamba,
Vilcanota, and Negra. Leader of first Peruvian ascent of
Huascarán, the highest peak in Peru

Tons of ice and rock tumbled down the mountain and fell into Laguna Pal-
cacocha on December 13, 1941, causing the lake to burst through its moraine
and flood the valley of Huaraz, killing twenty relatives of César Morales Arnao.

"Half of Huaraz disappeared," he said, "and 7,000 people died. After that,
I began some geological investigations in the mountains with my brothers to discover the origin of that kind of phenomenon. Naturally we had to climb."

The disaster and succeeding investigations led Morales Arnao to the mountains for several years after that. In 1951, he met members of a French-Belgian
expedition who gave him a sleeping bag, pack, and climbing shoes—his first quality
equipment.

Two years later, he was working on dams, securing them with safety dykes
to prevent other avalanches. "I worked with some Indian friends. They were strong,
very strong. In May, one group came from Mexico and they climbed the Huascarán. We met with them and they said, 'Why don't the Peruvians climb the
Huascarán?' Then my friends and I formed the *Grupo Andinista Cordillera Blanca*
[Cordillera Blanca Climbing Group], and I selected six people who were very
strong—three brothers Yanac, two brothers Mautino, and one Angeles. With them
I prepared the equipment. We borrowed from several different places. *El Commercio* [a major newspaper in Lima] gave us the money for the enterprise. Then
with good training, good personnel, and good spirit, we organized the climb on
the west route for the Glacier Raimondi, which was the normal route.

"I led the group from the beginning of the glacier to the col at 6,000 meters.
There I had to return to the valley to organize the newspaper coverage. I had to

give information to *El Commercio* and information to the people, and I gave orders to my boys every night at 7:30.

"I got a telescope in Yungay and Mancos. It was amazing, the reaction of the people. For the first time, the people saw lights and flashes. This was only the third climb on Huascarán. The first was the Germans in '32 and then, because of the [interruption of] the war, the Mexicans in '53, and the Peruvians in '53.

"On the fourth of August, my boys put the flag of Peru on the top of Huascarán. From the valley I arranged the telescopes, and all the people looked at my boys on the top of Huascarán. I allowed them to look for only one minute so other people could see. It was very exciting. A plane flew over, taking photographs. A lot of people went to the beginning of the glacier to give a reception to the six boys. They returned, and we went down, and in each town all the people were clapping and throwing flowers and money. *El Commercio* took some pictures and got some good information about us. It was in all the papers. We made speeches in Yungay, Mancos, and Huaraz. That night, the director of *El Commercio* called me and said, 'After this great adventure, we invite all the team to come to Lima to pass one week of celebrations.' I accepted in the name of my boys and we went to Lima.

"In Lima, they gave us lodging in the Hotel Bolivar. You see, these Indian boys never knew the water closet or other comforts of the Hotel Bolivar, such a nice place with all the best. Every day we had meetings in the Government Palace, in the Parliament, in several science institutions, in theaters. One company donated a plane and flew over the city with the boys. They had never seen a plane before.

"They walked in the street, not six boys, but forty or fifty always, because they were legends. They had lunch in the Bolivar and *El Commercio* paid for it. At the end of the week, on Sunday, we went to the Estadio Nacional [National Stadium]. The Estadio was only beginning its activities that year and we went to a football [soccer] game. In front of thousands of people, we made one Olympic lap around the track and all the people were cheering. After that, we returned to Huaraz and the boys returned to work.

"From that year on, the people looked at alpinists differently. Now they think it is normal to climb a mountain. Before that, they did not believe that people could stay on the glacier. Our flag lasted one week on top."

The association with that historic climb placed César Morales Arnao in a position of importance in relation to mountaineering in the Peruvian Andes. He was given a position in the Peruvian Institute of Sport, which later gave him the opportunity to make changes in the mountains he loves so well. He founded the Parque Nacional Huascarán (Huascarán National Park), two Peruvian climbing organizations, a speleological society, and a conservation group to protect the Inca Trail and other trails in the Peruvian Cordilleras. He also organized the *Revista Peruana de Andinismo y Glaciologia (Peruvian Review of Mountaineering and Glaciology)* and has been its only editor since 1952.

Morales Arnao holds a doctorate in journalism from the University of San Martin de Porres. He explained, "I like this kind of work because I am a journalist, and with this magazine I can promote my land. My land is the Cordillera Blanca because I was born in Huaraz. It is good for me to show the beauties of my land to other countries with this magazine. I send this magazine to all the alpine clubs and geographical associations, tourism groups, national parks, and wildlife organizations.

"Also, every year in the months of November, December, and January, I receive letters from every part of the world asking me about the condition of the mountains; it is my job to answer the questions. Because of this, I hope that every expedition, after they climb, will write one small report about the climb so we will know routes they make. Then I can make recommendations to other climbers about the problems. This year eighty expeditions came from sixteen countries, so this is much work.

"Every year interest in the Peruvian Andes is growing because we have a lot of very nice objectives in several places. People come to climb the mountains or go trekking, spelunking, skiing on the glaciers, skiing in the sand in the desert, surfing, rafting, kayaking, floating on the jungle rivers, hang gliding, horse riding, windsurfing. I must keep all this information."

The efforts of César Morales Arnao have changed the future of the mountains in Peru. They have also changed the attitudes of Peruvians toward visiting climbers, yet the Peruvians don't climb often themselves.

"There are several Peruvian clubs of mountaineering," Morales Arnao said, "but ordinarily, the Peruvian people don't like camping, outdoor activities, or climbing mountains. Maybe it is because the equipment is very expensive. Also, we were born in the lands near the peaks and always want to progress. We arrive in big cities looking for jobs. Maybe in our jobs we attain a superior standard of life and maybe we don't want to remember the earlier social problems, so we don't go back to that place. Peruvians do not have much desire for outdoor activities."

In his office at the Peruvian Institute of Sport, Morales Arnao for years has seen most of the expeditions headed for the Peruvian Andes. "At first, climbers were making easy routes. Now the alpinist wants very difficult routes with much sophisticated equipment. Before, we climbed for the pleasure of looking, of walking in the ice and seeing the rocks, looking at wildlife, and for pleasure, but in the last years people have forgotten this kind of value. Now the people want to make very difficult routes, very exclusive routes, and climbing is becoming more like a sport and this is against the end of mountaineering. Mountaineering pleasure is to see the natural, the creation of the mountains, the lakes, the trees, the animals. Maybe that has changed in mountaineering now. The equipment is more expensive so the biggest climbs are in the hands of a few people, the rich people. The character of the true alpinist is to be in the land, walking on the trails, climbing the mountains."

He compared climbing to a disease. "Climbers spend money and accept trouble to climb the mountain. They go home and five months later they are thinking about it again. This is the sickness of the alpinist. Because of this, we climb several mountains, not only one.

"I am an explorer. I began with the books of my ancestor, Don Antonio Raimondi. I read the books and I wanted to know these areas. The place that is difficult for people to reach, that place, I like to reach that place to see what kind of constitution it has. For that I climb."

Leigh Ortenburger

Born:

February 14, 1929, Norman, Oklahoma

Hometown:

Palo Alto, California

Occupation:

Statistician

Climbing Highlights:

Makalu (attempt). Major expeditions to the Cordillera Blanca of Peru in 1952, 1954, 1958, 1959, 1964, 1971, 1977, 1981, 1983, in which he climbed twenty-six peaks over 6,000 meters, including Chopicalqui, Huandoy, Huantsan, Chacraraju. Numerous first ascents in the Tetons of Wyoming. Wrote guidebook to the Tetons

Leigh Ortenburger has focused much of his climbing energy on two mountain ranges—the Tetons of Wyoming and the Cordillera Blanca of Peru. He has climbed most of the peaks in both ranges and has developed a more complete knowledge of the history and physical features of those two ranges than any other climber.

"The way I got involved with the Tetons was sort of strange," Ortenburger recalled. "When I was in high school I didn't have much homework, but my parents had the *Encyclopaedia Britannica* and I used to leaf through that. One night, I picked up the G volume and in the lower right hand corner of a right hand page was a paragraph on Grand Teton National Park. I had never heard of it and in there was a sentence which I can quote word for word. It said, 'Grand Teton is one of the most difficult peaks in the United States to climb.' I said 'Aha! I'd better go check that out!' So I hitchhiked out. I was nineteen at the time and had never seen a rope."

By 1952, he had climbed extensively in the Tetons and was part of one of the first expeditions to the Cordillera Blanca in Peru. He eventually participated in ten trips there because, in those mountains, "you can find any difficulty that you want from literally a walk up to something that you can't climb. There is a real attraction in the challenge of high altitude. Altitude, it seems to me, is another dimension, just like difficulty is. Some people can climb difficult rock and not acclimatize. There have been some famous examples of that. Other people can acclimatize and not do very well on difficult rock. It's another dimension in climbing. You can't get that sort of experience in the United States, this challenge of altitude.

"Of course, the mountain scenery down there is fantastic. One of the great features is that up high it is a very clear, dry atmosphere and if you happen to hit some decent weather, it's beautiful. At night, it's just a deadly silence up there. That's an attractive thing. No sounds. No civilization. You are completely removed from all that. I can remember some morning starts at three A.M. that were perfectly still."

For Ortenburger, there are two important factors about climbing. "Part of it has to do with the sense of exploration. I'm interested in seeing what's there, in seeing what's on the other side of the mountain, or the details of a certain route. It's the lure of the unknown. The other aspect is that climbing is a challenge to see what you can do, to see if you can overcome some of these obstacles that nature confronts you with. It's hard to make much more out of it than that. Certainly I object to the public view of climbers as great heroes, great supermen. Climbing on television and in the newspapers is portrayed as a heroic sport, taking great dangers, risking lives, and all this nonsense. Proper climbing is not like that at all in my opinion. I do have one quote that is a favorite and it is attributed to the arctic explorer Fridtjof Nansen. It says, 'Adventure is the mark of incompetence.' In other words, if you get yourself into an adventurous situation, you've done something wrong. If you know what you are doing, then things proceed in a straightforward manner. If you come back with frozen toes, then you've screwed up. The very worst thing that can happen to you is to have to be rescued. You have really blown it if you get yourself into that situation.

"There are a lot of people who ignore some standards of safety and say, 'Well, if I fall off, just let the body lie there,' and they ignore that fact that it just doesn't work that way. In a national park, there is no way that the government or the people or society will permit a body to just sit up there. One needs some sense of social responsibility, which some climbers don't have.

"But climbing is a foolish business. There is no earthly reason for doing it. You can get killed up there, and much of the purpose of climbing is to minimize the dangers. Some people are content to go under ice falls and for the most part, but not always, they get away with it.

"Climbing is something that one should do only because there is something inside you that says you want to do it. In no way should it be done because somebody tells you to do it. The real climbers are a very independent bunch of people who have this inner push. They are not conformists, to put it mildly. They are a separate bunch of individuals and within that group there is quite a wide range from the real macho, arrogant types to the quiet, unassuming, exceedingly competent climber. There was a time that I thought that if you were a climber, you were necessarily a really fine person, a great guy. Unfortunately, that isn't true.

"I do think climbers are better than the average person on the street, in some sense. One unfortunate aspect is that there is still widely practiced competition with other climbers. That, I think, is absolutely the wrong way to go at climbing and yet I don't doubt that it has led to the development of some of these very difficult climbs. Competition can't be the reason for climbing, to show that you can climb something that Joe over there can't or that you can do it faster or that you can do it with fewer pitons or fewer nuts. Much of that developed in Yosemite, but because of it, they developed the state of the art in rock climbing. No doubt. I think, given a choice, I'd rather be non-competitive and climb things of lesser difficulty than be forced to be competitive in order to do the hard climbs.

"You try to improve all the time, but I would view it as improvement rather than competition. Many of today's climbers seem to live on competition, but it's not the essense of what climbing's about. Climbing will go along quite well without it."

Forty years of climbing have left Ortenburger with a broad perspective on the sport's development. He has watched as the difficulty of the standard climbs has gone ever upward toward more and more difficult climbs. He remembers when "most climbing was done by students, teachers, who studied or taught in the winter and came out in the summer with very little training. By the end of the summer, they might be in shape. Now, climbers are working out on Nautilus machines and doing all kinds of exercises all winter long and are in vastly better physical condition than we ever used to be, and because of that, they are doing things that are more difficult than we used to do. World records and Olympic records improve very slowly and it follows that climbing difficulty really can't get much beyond where it is now or if it does, it will go slowly. I think the future of climbing will be what it's always been—that the bulk of it will be done by people who are not the hot shots, but people who are doing minimal roped climbing. This is where a majority of the action is and there are many people who get a lot of enjoyment out of doing that. I think that is going to continue to be the main-stream of climbing.

"It's hard to say where the super-technical climbing is going to lead. Equip-ment makes a big difference. I've seen huge changes in equipment. When I started there weren't down jackets. Such a thing as an ice screw hadn't been invented. What I think is really one of the great inventions for snow and ice climbing, and which doesn't get much press, is the dead man. This is one of the great technical breakthroughs, yet people don't talk about it much. What it permits one to do is climb routes safely that we used to do, knowing full well that this ice axe belay that we were trying to use very likely wouldn't hold if somebody fell. But a dead man will hold a fall and that makes all the difference in safety. You can do those things and survive.

"It's different from rock. Just because a person can do difficult rock doesn't mean he can do difficult snow and ice. I have to say something about a bias of mine. Today, technical ice climbing is viewed as going up nearly vertical waterfalls on your front points with a couple of ice tools in your hands and that's the living end. I believe it is very difficult, but on a big mountain that is not the type of difficulty the mountain puts in front of you. In particular in Peru, because it is so dry and because it is high altitude, you get what is called cheese ice. The Germans called it that. This is an ice that is full of holes and the water sublimes away. It doesn't melt, it just evaporates, so you get this stuff that is nearly vertical and it won't hold your weight. So this business of front-pointing up on nice ice doesn't apply. Instead, what you end up doing is cutting a step above your head and by

the time you have it down to the foot level, it may hold your weig
true nature of some of the climbing on the high peaks."

In 1961, Ortenburger was with Sir Edmund Hillary on a scier
taineering expedition to Makalu in the Himayalas. The purpose of the expe...
was to attempt Makalu and, at the same time, perform valuable scientific research
on high altitude physiology. The climb and research were both hampered when
a New Zealander became ill at 27,000 feet. Ortenburger gave up his summit
chance to aid in the rescue of his fellow climber.

That was his only climb in the Himalayas because "it is such an expensive
organizational and political problem whereas, in Peru, you just pack up and go.
The peaks in Peru aren't as high, but certainly you can get all the difficulty you
want. I guess I just never had the energy to fight all the politics and the fundraising,
to go around with my hand out to support the climbing I wanted to do. To me
that doesn't make sense. Why should somebody else pay for you having fun?
Maybe the manufacturers who make the big donations should, to some small
extent, because climbing does support them."

Climbing in Peru was exciting for Ortenburger. He recalled reaching the summit of Huandoy Oeste. "I didn't stand on the top. It was a triangular pyramid of
snow with three steep faces, so I got to the point where I could reach up and
whack the snow off the top with my ice axe. It wasn't the sort of place where
you wanted to stand. We were camped at the saddle of Huandoy and the other
two fellows were a little slower in getting ready and the route from the saddle is
pretty straight forward, just sort of walking uphill on the snow and ice, and I said,
'I'll go ahead and make steps and I'm sure you guys will catch up.' I got up to
the upper saddle and I didn't see them, so I continued up the final ridge and I
just sort of kept going, not intending to go all the way to the summit by myself.
I could see a cornice on the right and I knew I had to go to the left to avoid being
over that cornice. I finally reached the summit and looked back down, and there
were my steps right out over thin air. I hadn't gone far enough down to the left.
I thought I had, but when I looked down, I could see that I had been noticeably
out on the cornice. These mountains present a whole different set of problems
and if you climb very much in Peru, you sometimes have to do those sorts
of things."

Facing difficulties is inherent in climbing and Ortenburger likes to sum up the
challenges by saying, "One's best climb is not always one's most enjoyable. You
appreciate a climb more if the conditions were adverse. It's one thing to climb
the Exum Ridge [on the Grand Teton] on a sunny day and it's another thing to
lead the Friction Pitch when it's got sleet on it and it's running water. You remember the hard days more easily than the good days. The challenge and the
sense of exploration are important—more the sense of exploration for me. If you
are the first person to visit a place, you've got to poke around and look and think."

In 1952, Lionel Terray, a Frenchman, made the first ascent of a major peak
of the Cordillera Blanca called Huantsan. Ortenburger completed the second ascent in 1958 and called it his most satisfying climb.

"There is an additional satisfaction if a climb is the result of only your own

:forts. If somebody else has led half the pitches, it's still a worthwhile thing to have done, but you didn't do it by yourself. On Huantsan, I was with a porter. He was a very strong fellow, but not given to leading, so when we reached the summit, I felt that I had done most of it. It was quite satisfying.

"On the way up Huantsan, there is a section of blue ice on the ridge which was surprising because it doesn't happen very often down there. On the way down, we found one of Terray's ice pitons. He had rappelled it whereas I cut steps up it. Nowadays, nobody would do that and Terray didn't either.

"There is a school of thought that says if you climb up you should climb down. Terray front-pointed up and rappelled down. We cut steps up and we climbed down. Which was the better of the two? It's not obvious to me. They are different. Stepcutting is almost a thing of the past. On a big mountain, step-cutting assures you of a way down. You can come down at night. I've come down many mountains safely this way.

"Another safety feature that is considered taboo for great alpine style is the fixed rope. I could point to any number of climbers who lived because of fixed ropes. Lionel Terray is a good example of that on Mt. Huntington. Coming down Chacaraju, we had a fixed rope in. Tom Frost and Dan Doody and I were coming down and Doody slipped and was saved by the fixed rope. We came down the ridge in one full day and a blizzard came up as we were doing the last part. It was about ten P.M. or perhaps midnight and if we hadn't had that rope, I really have doubts about our getting down. You have to experience things like this to understand this ethical thing of not using fixed ropes. There is a place for fixed ropes if you want to live. I have some strong feelings about the fads and 'ethics' of climbing.

"But I'm a bit out of step. For example, I may be the last living climber to use the body rappel. I believe that it is faster, simpler, and has fewer points of potential failure. I even use it on a free rappel. I may be a bit out of date on some of my beliefs, but I'm still alive and I've done a fair amount of climbing."

Glenn Exum

Born:
June 24, 1911, Topaz, Idaho
Hometown:
Moose, Wyoming
Occupation:
Retired teacher, operator of
Exum Guide Service
Climbing Highlights:
Grand Teton, Exum Ridge (first ascent, solo); Grand Teton, East
Ridge (second ascent); Grand Teton, North Face (second ascent);
Thor Mountain, East Face (first ascent); Matterhorn (first solo
American ascent); and many climbs throughout the Tetons as
a guide

When Glenn Exum looked across the gap at the end of Wall Street and saw
the 1,500-foot drop in front of him, he hesitated. After all, it was only his second
climb. Moreover, he was alone and the route above had never been climbed
before. And his size nine feet were inside Paul Petzoldt's size eleven and a half
football cleats.

Eight feet of open space separated Exum and the main ridge. He looked at
the blank wall and didn't think he could climb across. He knew he couldn't jump
so he ran back down the Wall Street ledge to yell at Petzoldt.

The two had met in the summer of 1930 when Exum went to Jackson Hole
to play in a dance band at Jenny Lake. He worked during the days building the
lower portion of the Garnet Canyon trail for the Park Service. He also worked on
a road grader building a road from Jenny Lake to the north end of Leigh Lake.
Petzoldt also worked on this crew.

"Before I met Paul, I never even thought of climbing," Exum said. "When I
looked at the mountains, I wondered how anyone could even do that, because I
was very young and hadn't been exposed to anything like that. One day, he said,
'Ex, how would you like to climb the Grand Teton?' "

The two made an ascent of the Owen-Spalding route and Exum thought that
would be the end of his climbing. But Petzoldt had different ideas.

"I had finished high school and was going to Pocatello to the University and
found out Paul was going there, so we became friends and continued our friendship
in the winter. The next summer we came out and I was playing in the band at
Jenny Lake and working on the trail. Paul said, 'Ex, I think I'm going to make a
guide out of you.' I said, 'This is rather sudden. I've never climbed except last

summer with you and I don't know anything about it.' He said, 'That's all right, you have the aptitude.' "

Petzoldt gave Exum the football shoes and they set off on Exum's first guiding trip. They were to take Mr. and Mrs. Fred Whittenburger of Vienna, Austria, up the Owen-Spalding route. They had climbed past the Lower Saddle and the Belly Roll Almost, when Petzoldt called to Exum, "Come up here, Ex, I want to show you something."

He pointed to a slanting ledge he had seen from the Middle Teton in the mid-1920s. He had never been over to scout the ledge, but believed that it would lead to the summit. He knew that Robert Underhill of the American Alpine Club (who Exum called "the best technical rock climber of his time"), Phil Smith, a seasonal ranger in Grand Teton National Park, and Frank Truslow of the Harvard Mountaineering Club were attempting a climb on the southeast ridge that day.

"Paul had sort of a competitive nature," Exum explained, "and he'd seen this big ledge earlier. He said, 'Run over there and take a look at it. If it doesn't look good, call and we'll wait for you and you can go on with us.' "

That was how Glenn Exum found himself at the exposed end of Wall Street by himself on his second climb. He recounted the incident. "That day the wind was blowing from the southwest and I got up there to the end of that ledge and it scared me to death, so I ran all the way down to the bottom of Wall Street and I yelled, 'Petzoldt, it doesn't look very good.' Then I ran back up again and looked at it again." He laughed. "It looked worse, so I ran back down screaming."

In the back of his mind, Exum had an idea that the route would go, but his inexperience just wouldn't let him commit to the climb. But then "after seven times of running up and down, I finally got up there and saw those little handholds and the boulder, and I decided if I got up high enough and lunged hard enough, I could jump across that thing and land on that big boulder. So that was what I did. When I was on the other side, I knew I was never going to make it back. There was no way I could possibly get back over there. I did have the advantage of jumping down and not straight across. I did have a little rope, a clothesline rope. I never even took it off. All I had was a sweatshirt and Paul's football shoes.

"As soon as I got across, I screamed again and Petzoldt never did hear me. I was really frightened. I could hear Smith, Truslow, and Underhill giving signals and talking, but they couldn't hear me. I yelled a few more times and finally decided I had better conserve my energy and start climbing. I took off and stayed right on the ridge and went all the way to the top.

"I was up there an hour and a half before Petzoldt got there with the Austrians. I saw Paul, with his bushy eyebrows, come up over the edge, and he started running. He forgot he was tied to the Austrians and they were just hitting the ground every once in awhile." He laughed at the memory. "He grabbed me and gave me a big bear hug and said, 'Do you know what you have done?' I didn't really have any perception of what I had done because it was only my second climb. We sat there and signed the register and I wrote a description of where I thought I had gone.

"Pretty soon we heard the jingling of pitons and Underhill and his companions came up. It was a significant day, because on that day, July 15, 1931, there were three parties that came up three different routes and two of them were new routes. The east ridge was the only other route, and Underhill had led that in 1929, so he had led two of the routes. Every route that had ever been climbed on the Grand Teton was represented there that day. Just ten days later, Underhill and [Fritiof] Fryxell climbed the north ridge."

Exum enjoyed his time on the summit with the other parties, but he had a problem. He had to play in the band that night, so he left the others and started down. From above he heard Petzoldt yelling down. "He was shouting, 'Exum, you're crazy to do this,' but I thought he had said, 'Exum, any old lady could do this,' and it made me so mad I ran all the way down to Jenny Lake." Exum laughed again.

Exum's climb was not the only ascent of that route that day. On the way down, with the Austrians waiting for him at the Lower Saddle, Petzoldt went over to see the ledge Exum had described. He took out his rope, lassoed the boulder, crossed the gap with his arm over the rope, and made the second ascent of the route. This technique was standard procedure for several years following, and the location became known as Lasso Ledge.

After this experience, the two formed the Petzoldt-Exum Climbing School and worked together for several years. "We'd just go out in the campground and find some guy," Exum explained. "If he could walk, we'd throw a rope on him and go. We didn't have any pitons or anything. We just went down to the blacksmith's shop in Jackson and had him take a piece of old scrap iron and punch a hole in it and that's what we used. Those things are strung all over the mountains and I think you can still find them on the east face of Mt. Moran."

Later, Petzoldt became interested in agriculture and moved on. In 1956, Exum got a concession from Grand Teton National Park and formed Exum Mountain Guides. His work as a music teacher in the winter had given him a definite philosophy about working with people.

"I worked out a system in my teaching that was very successful. I had about forty boys in a chorus and I said, 'Look, I know any one of you boys could tear down this school, but instead of tearing it down, why don't we go out and build it up. Why don't we go out and pick up some of the paper and clean the place up. I'm not going to herd you around. I'm going to let you elect a captain and herd yourselves.' Before long they got so tough on each other I had to ask them to slack up. We worked on a merit system. They learned punctuality and respect."

Exum combined this attitude about working with people with a basic feeling that "people by nature are good climbers, every one of them. We are born to climb. Watch a little child, a baby. They climb beautifully."

Exum worked with his guides to develop a system of bringing out the best in his clients. The school quickly developed a reputation and the list of guides who have worked for Exum over the years could easily fill a page in *Who's Who in American Mountaineering*, if such a thing existed.

He has seen literally thousands of climbers come through his guide service. He noted, "I think climbing does have a magnet to it in drawing very unusual people. I think if you would survey people who generally climb, most of them are highly educated. Over the years, we've had more medical doctors than any other profession here. We have lots of academic people."

Exum sold the guide service in 1978 when he was facing one of the most difficult climbs of his life, an uphill battle against cancer. He had operations in 1977 and 1978 and the doctor told him he would never climb again.

By 1981, however, Exum was doing better and received a letter asking about the possibility of completing a fiftieth anniversary climb of the Grand. His doctor approved (and later accompanied him on the climb), and after a good training program, Exum decided to try.

Two film crews and a host of former guides and climbing partners arrived. The group camped at the Lower Saddle on July 14 and set out the next morning to climb. Exum moved well and changed rope partners with each pitch so he could climb with all his friends. His blood pressure actually decreased on the mountain and he climbed to the summit with a lifetime of friends, exactly fifty years after his lonely and frightening first ascent.

On the summit, he talked briefly with his wife via radio-telephone and his friends gave him a gold-plated Chouinard ice axe and a silver belt buckle that read "Exum Ridge 50."

On the descent, he decided to stay one more night at the Lower Saddle. "I knew I would never get up there again," he explained. "We had had a perfect climb, and you don't want to keep singing after you lose your voice.

"I carried that hut up there in the sixties and wanted to stay just one more time. Some guy knocked on the door and said, 'Would you come out here and take a picture with us, and sign our certificates of ascent?' Two weeks later, I got a letter that said, 'I am enclosing a picture taken at the base camp on the Grand. I am also enclosing a picture taken at the base camp on the moon.' It was signed, 'Your grateful friend from above, James B. Irwin.' I met the guy and never even knew who he was."

After his initiation to the sport of climbing, Exum devoted his life to teaching it to others. "Climbing, in my mind, is a sport, but it's a release, sort of like dry fly fishing. You get a release from yourself.

"I have loved climbing, and the reason is that if you are up there and having a beautiful day and everyone is clicking and a few cumulus clouds are sprinkled around and everyone is moving and handling the rope right and the air is clear and you can see forever, well, I think that is really almost an unmatchable experience. It is almost sacred."

From the window of his home in Moose, Exum has a clear view of the Grand Teton and the ridge that bears his name. "I feel it's a monument. I feel so undeserving to have something that beautiful named after me, but my son and my grandson have the same name also. When I look back at it, it was just a fluke. Nobody knew it would be the most perfect place for guiding. I just happened to get up there first. It could have been somebody else. It is a much greater monument than a guy could ever have in a cemetery. I'll never be in a cemetery. I want to be thrown up into the air and just drift down and become part of the world."

Scott Heywood ►
on winter ascent
in the
Snowy Range.
(Scott Heywood)

◄ Jim Whittaker.
(Dianne Roberts)

Rick Ridgeway under the ►
Rostrum Roof, Yosemite.
(Ridgeway Collection)

◄Dick Bass at the summit of Mt. Everest. (Dick Bass)

▲ Jan Bien Conn at age 13, climbing her house. "It was more fun than sedately walking up the stairs," she explained. (Jan Conn)

Jack Durrance with rappelling rope in the Sawtooth Mountains. ▼ (Dick Durrance)

▲ Adams Carter in Peru in the late 1970s. (H. Adams Carter)

◄ Jack Tackle during first winter ascent of the North Face of Grand Teton. (Alex Lowe)

▲ Arlene Blum trekking in the Himalaya. (Arlene Blum)

Brad and Barbara Washburn on the ► summit of Mt. Bertha, Alaska, July 31, 1940, on their first climb together three months after their marriage. (Bradford Washburn)

Chris Bonington ▶
climbing in
the Lake District of
northern England.
(Chris Bonington)

Yvon Chouinard climbing
in a chimney at Red Rocks, Nevada.
▼ **(Yvon Chouinard)**

▲ Al Read in Nepal after leading
the expedition that made the first
ascent of Gaurishankar, 1979.
(Al Read)

▲ Leigh Ortenburger at age 23 on his first expedition to Peru in 1952. **(Leigh Ortenburger)**

▲ T. I. M. Lewis at Czech Film Festival 1982. **(P. A. Lewis)**

Glenn Exum on the Exum Ridge of the Grand Teton. **(Exum Mountain Guides)** ▼

César Morales Arnao in the trekking camp near Quebrada Santa Cruz in the Cordillera Blanca of Peru, 1972. ▼ **(César Morales Arnao)**

▲ Jeff Lowe. **(Michael Kennedy)**

▲ Royal Robbins on the direct route, Northwest Face of Half Dome, 1963. **(Dick McCracken)**

▲ Jim Bridwell on Everest Grand Circle Expedition with Nuptse in background. **(Jim Bridwell)**

Galen Rowell with his dog, ► Khumbu, in the John Muir Wilderness, High Sierra, California. **(Barbara Cushman Rowell)**

◄ Finis Mitchell in the Wind River Mountains of Wyoming. **(Finis Mitchell)**

Warren Harding and ►
Beryl Knauth on the summit
of Wall of the Early
Morning Light (Dawn Wall), 1970.
(Fresno Bee)

◄ Patrik Callis bouldering on "Ode to Ester" at the Grove near Bozeman, Montana. **(Tom Jungst)**

Alison Osius on "Toxic" ►
(5.11c) at Smith Rock, Oregon.
(Greg Epperson)

◄ Todd Skinner
leading "Bombs over
Tripoli" (5.12)
at City of the Rocks
in Idaho. **(Bill Hatcher)**

Lynn Hill. ►
(Greg Epperson)

Yvon Chouinard

Born:
November 9, 1938, Lewiston, Maine

Hometown:
Ventura, California

Occupation:
Owner, outdoor equipment
and clothing companies

Climbing Highlights:
North American Wall (first ascent), Muir Wall (first ascent), the
Nose (first hammerless ascent), Mt. Watkins South Face (first
ascent), West Buttress of South Howser Tower (first ascent),
Southwest Face of Fitzroy (first ascent), North Face of Mt. Edith
Cavell, and numerous ice climbs and first ascents in the Tetons
and Shawangunks, and many others

Yvon Chouinard settled into an easy chair in the living room of his log home,
just south of Moose, Wyoming. He looked at the rustic beauty around him and
said, "I've wanted this all my life."

One thing a person learns quickly about Yvon Chouinard is that, when he
wants something, he usually gets it. His life's story is one of success after success
in what appear to be divergent interests.

To anyone who is interested in mountain climbing, the name Yvon Chouinard
evokes thoughts of a small man who was able to power his way up some of the
toughest first ascents of his generation. To someone interested in business, the
Chouinard name is a rags-to-riches story of a high school dropout who built a
multi-million dollar outdoor equipment company.

Chouinard first developed an interest in climbing when he was a member of
a falconry club in Los Angeles. He learned climbing techniques to enable him to
reach hawk and falcon nests. "One day out at Stony Point near L.A., I was just
practicing rappelling down this chimney and I couldn't believe it," he recalled.
"There was some guy climbing up. That was where I first got the idea of not just
rappelling down, but actually climbing up."

With his curiosity piqued, Chouinard spent time with a fellow falconer, Don
Prentice, who taught him how to use ropes and hardware. The summer he was
sixteen, Chouinard met Prentice and a group of climbers in the Wind River Mountains of Wyoming and climbed in the Gannett Peak area.

Later, Chouinard went to the Tetons and spent time hanging around Jenny
Lake. There he met several Dartmouth climbers, but Chouinard said, "These guys

wouldn't climb with you unless you said that you had lots of experience, so I told them I had lots of experience."

They took Chouinard on a climb, an ascent of Templeton's Crack on Symmetry Spire. After all the Dartmouth climbers had failed to lead the hardest section of the climb, they handed the hardware to Chouinard and told him to lead it.

"That was my first real lead," he noted. "Then I spent the rest of the summer in the Tetons climbing around."

That was the beginning of a great climbing career. In California, Chouinard completed two first ascents on the 3,000-foot face of El Capitan, the North American Wall, and the Muir Wall. He also made the first pitonless ascent of the Nose. He traveled all over the United States, climbing new routes, and today his name appears in almost every climber's guidebook that covers mountain ranges in the United States.

"At different points in my life I have sort of specialized in each facet of climbing," Chouinard explained. "For a year or two, I did a lot of slab friction climbs. Then I did a year or two of crack climbs. There was a period where I did a lot of ice climbing for about ten years. What I prefer more than anything else is mixed climbing, the alpine climbing. About the only place you can get really good mixed climbing is in the winter or in the Alps."

His pioneering efforts on ice drew much attention; he was the first to climb so many ice walls and frozen waterfalls that people began to search him out for information about ice climbing. The result was his only book, *Climbing Ice*. Chouinard spent seven years writing the book, and in the introduction wrote, "Climbing is easy, writing is difficult."

"I'm trying to avoid any more writing," he said. "Time seems to be more and more valuable to me and writing takes a lot of time. When I was younger, I had a lot of things I wanted to get off my chest. I don't any more. I sort of have a hopeless feeling about being able to change anything. At one time, you felt like you were instrumental in changing the whole climbing world, like limiting the use of pitons, but it was temporary. You go to El Cap now and you'll see climbers and they have a full rack of chocks, but they also have a full rack of pitons, just in case the chocks don't get them up. They've got ten times more equipment than we ever did. They've got porta-ledges. You know, they'll get up El Cap no matter what. I don't think there has been a hammerless ascent since we did it over ten years ago."

In his progression as a climber, Chouinard naturally graduated to bigger mountains. He made ascents in the Canadian Rockies and then moved on to the Himalayas. He experienced dangerous situations, but his successes continued until one day, in 1980, on a glacier in China.

"I've had a lot of close calls in my life. I've been in car wrecks where the car was just demolished and I was thrown out and was miraculously unscathed. I've taken big leader falls—a 160-foot leader fall on a 9-mil. rope—and ended up in the middle of the air with just a cut leg and that was all. A lot of times I really thought, 'This is it.' But I was caught in an avalanche in China and I think I almost went over the edge. It was different in that it was such a long and hopeless experience. It was 1,500-feet long and the whole time I was tumbling and going over 40-foot cliffs with the avalanche nearly stopped. I was struggling to get the rope off and it started up again and went over another cliff and once again I accepted the fact that I was dead. I got hit on the head and woke up and the guy next to me was dead and another guy had a broken back and the other guy was bleeding all over. I think the difference was that, every other time I've had a close call, right afterwards I felt elated and went around smelling flowers and it was great to be alive. After this, we were in severe depression for a long time afterwards, partly because a good friend [ABC cameraman Jonathon Wright] had died. But I also think we went over that line and actually died and came back, because reading stories about clinical deaths where people have gone over the other side and come back, they're in a real depression for a long time. That's what happened to us. It's quite a different experience than I've ever had before. Both [Rick] Ridgeway and I agree that we have no desire to go above 25,000 feet. I'll just stick to mountains below that. Above that you have too many things that are out of your control."

Chouinard became quiet for a moment, reflecting on what he had said, and then he continued. "I think I had accepted death and come back—I don't know. I can't explain it. Other people have said that when they've gone over to the other side it was nice and peaceful and very pleasurable and all of a sudden, they are jerked back into the real life and they resented it. We didn't go that far, but we were depressed. I was depressed for three weeks after that. For some of the other guys it was much longer. This was the only time I've ever put a limit on it. I mean, I've had friends get killed in the mountains and I've never used that as an excuse to say, 'I'm never going to go climbing again, because too many of my friends have been killed.' That's sort of an excuse to get out of climbing and I've never done that. I don't think I'd ever stop climbing, just do different kinds, because you can control the risk in most climbing. There are just some things that you can't, particularly with snow. You could be the world's greatest avalanche expert and if you're in the mountains much, you're going to get avalanched. You can't control it 100 percent."

That idea of not being able to completely control the elements on a climb is important to Chouinard, because the feeling of risk only adds to his reasons for climbing.

"I think I enjoy risk-type sports. I think there is a certain challenge involved in it and it's pleasurable. I mean, I don't do any of these things just to prove a point. I wouldn't be doing them unless they were really enjoyable. But I think they are even more enjoyable because there is an element of risk. Not that I want to go out and purposely risk my neck or anything. It isn't that you are doing that, because after a while you get really good at these things.

"What is a big risk for the average person is a small risk for you, really. But you're right there on the edge and it adds a tremendous amount to the excitement of the sport. You don't get that in, say, windsurfing. Windsurfing is a high-excitement sport and you get that feeling of speed and motion and your body directly controlling this fairly simple machine, but there is no risk involved and that is a big difference. That's why climbing only appeals to the one percent, or to the one-tenth of one percent. Most people will not accept a sport that has risk.

"During the sixties, all the risk-type sports were very popular, because everybody was rebelling against their parents, or rebelling against the whole system. But those days are over. This is the day of conservatism. This is the day of everybody going to school and becoming attorneys and Young Republicans. Risks don't have anything to do with their lives. It's another generation.

"We go through alternate generations. Right now the kids that are out doing sports are the children of the parents of the sixties. They don't want to be dopers and run around hitchhiking and living on fifty cents a day. No, they're Yuppies. They're the cleanies. Climbing and that kind of sport doesn't appeal to these people. I'm happy to see that. I'm happy to see that climbing is going back. The only people getting into climbing are the geeks again.

"It bothered me in the seventies when the average guy on the street was running around with a carabiner hanging off his belt. Now you get on the good Class V rivers and all you see are the geeks. You get back into the mountains and there are the real individuals and the people who don't fit in. I've been a geek all my life, but I do fit in. In fact, I enjoy fitting into a lot of different classic scenes. It doesn't matter if it's a cocktail party in Buenos Aires in tuxes—I mean that's classic in itself—or if it's sitting around in the dirt at Camp IV. I love classic scenes."

The sporting side of climbing was only one aspect for Chouinard. Early in his climbing career, he realized that much of the equipment he was using was inadequate and he saw ways of making it better. He set up a shop in a garage and started making mountain climbing equipment and selling his products in Yosemite Valley. Before long, people were asking him for more pieces of equipment than he could make. He decided to take the first of several business risks, and hired climbing friends to help him. The new business was a success. The small shop in Ventura, California, expanded and became the Great Pacific Ironworks, one of the leading manufacturers of climbing hardware in the world.

He also saw another problem in the climbing world. Not only was the hardware lacking, but the clothing that climbers wore was usually Army surplus or converted ski clothing. He set about designing clothing specifically for climbers and developed the Patagonia line, now sold around the world.

Being an equipment manufacturer suits Chouinard just fine, because the research necessary to produce top-quality products lets him be involved daily in tennis, diving, surfing (his favorite sport), kayaking, and climbing. "It's what I enjoy doing, plus it's my work," he said. "I have to do that to get ideas to design equipment and to design clothing."

Chouinard sees similarities between the satisfactions he gets from outdoor sports and from his business ventures. "I enjoy doing creative things. I don't enjoy rock climbing where somebody has gone ahead of me with a chalk bag and every handhold is marked out. That's climbing by the numbers. I can't stand that. I want to pick my own way. I think designing functional clothing and equipment gives me an outlet for creativity. So it seems to me that if I can go out kayaking and be thinking about how to improve a paddling jacket, I'm in heaven. That's great."

Being involved in the equipment industry, Chouinard has noticed the drift toward more specialization in the climbing world. He explained, "The great majority of climbers in the United States are sport climbers, rock climbers, and they only do 30- or 40-foot routes. They work on them all day and they are extremely difficult. It's more of a gymnastic type of thing. It has nothing to do with mountains, only the fact that the rocks came from mountains. It's like modern agriculture where the land only supports the chemicals to grow the vegetables. I mean, these people who are climbing on these rocks have no love of mountains or mountaineering or any of that stuff. It's strictly a gymnastic, very egocentric type of thing like a triathlon. That type of climbing is going to get more and more difficult and more specialized and you're going to have to climb year-round, year after year after year, and work out six hours a day on gymnastic equipment and spend the other two hours of the day climbing."

His work with equipment has also led Chouinard to the conviction that "technical development is killing the sport. With some climbing shoes now, the rubber is getting stickier and stickier and it turns a 5.10 route into a 5.8. You can take a pair of climbing shoes and put a sixteenth of an inch strip of surgical rubber on the bottom and you can walk up any extreme slab climb in the world. It destroys it. It throws the whole rating system away, which would be fine if there were harder and harder slab climbs to do. A 5.7 climber can get these new shoes and do a 5.10 and say 'God, I'm a 5.10 climber.' He's just completely deluded himself. I see that as a sad situation. At least he should admit that he cheated on the climb. And that's going to get worse and worse. Where's it going to stop? I mean, I could come out with a shoe with surgical rubber on the bottom, but it's just people deluding themselves."

The current type of climbing that Chouinard finds "really impressive" is the alpine-style ascents of large walls in the Himalayas. He prefers to see that style of climbing as opposed to the large siege climbs with full-scale expeditions.

"I'm a little pessimistic about [the future of] climbing myself," he confessed. "There seems to be less and less freedom involved in it. It's getting tougher and tougher to avoid following in someone else's footsteps. Like women climbers now are all really proud of themselves for being very close to the standards of men, but all they're doing is following these chalk trails. They're not going around doing new routes. Out of all the climbers around, there are just one or two in each area that are doing anything new and the rest are just—even though they're climbing at a very high standard—they're just doing what everybody else has done. I see that as kind of a sad case. I feel like I was extremely fortunate in being in the right place at the right time, because you could look around and see nothing but opportunities for new routes. You could go to Yosemite and all these walls had no routes on them at all. That was pretty amazing. We had no idea how easy we had it or I would have done a lot more first ascents." He laughed.

In his book, *Climbing Ice*, Chouinard wrote, "Climbing is a symptom of post-industrial man." He explained this statement by saying that in past years the

Sherpas thought climbers were crazy for leaving their nice homes and cars and coming to the mountains to seek challenge and a sense of being alive. The Sherpas didn't need to leave their homes to do that. They would have rather gone to the luxury of the homes and cars the climbers left behind. Chouinard feels that people who have been removed from direct contact with the earth have a stronger need to climb than people who have remained close to the soil. He said, "You don't see farmers as climbers. You see city people. Farmers don't need to climb."

Chouinard has received many letters from young people who are interested in climbing. They sometimes ask him if they should drop out of school and take up climbing. He often tells them to go ahead and drop, but be sure that climbing is exactly what they want before they make the decision. His attitude about school is that it "isn't that important. I'm keeping my kids out of school as long as I can. I think it's more important for them to learn outside of school and to develop their own character without having to bow to peer pressure."

He feels the only reason to stay in school is if a person wants to do something that requires a specified level of education, like becoming a doctor. Otherwise, he feels that the time could be better spent pursuing the desired activity.

"I dropped out of school and some of the most successful people I know dropped out of school, because they knew exactly what they wanted to do and it wasn't going to school. I see the time I spent in algebra as the biggest waste of time in my life. The only real value of these classes is that they develop your mind, but you can develop your mind in a lot of different ways."

Chouinard found those ways to develop his mind within himself and he has found that he has been his own best motivator and competitor throughout his life. He avoids overt competition.

"I play tennis, but I don't play in any tournaments, and as soon as anybody I'm playing with starts throwing his racquet or yelling about bad calls, I get away from that. I'm there by myself, hitting the ball, and it's coming back at me from somebody else, but I'm not too concerned about beating the other guy. I'm more concerned with my own strokes. I definitely avoid one-on-one competition. I don't like it and I don't do well with it. When I was a kid I was the best baseball player in grammar school, but when it would come time for a game I would just clutch up and couldn't do anything. Most climbers I know are exactly the same way. If they had to do what they do in front of a crowd, they would just clutch up and look like idiots."

Chouinard sees a relationship between his successes in the climbing and business worlds. "I think risk is important. You only get out of something what you put into it and the fact that you are willing to risk something means that you are going to get a lot more out of it. I don't care if it's a great financial risk or a physical risk. All of these risk-type sports are more satisfying because you put more on the line as far as your personal growth goes. People who take risks on a daily basis are more successful people, both mentally and physically, and, I think, are more content. I'm a happy man. There's no way I'm going to stop taking risks. Whatever confidence I have comes from striving and I know that and I'm not going to sit back in my rocking chair and take it easy."

74

Naoe Sakashita

Born:

February 6, 1948, Tokyo, Japan

Hometown:

Tokyo, Japan

Occupation:

Outdoor equipment distributor

Climbing Highlights:

Annapurna II (1973), Jannu (North Face, 1976), Russian Speed Climbing Championships (1978), Dru (West Face, 1978), Kanchenjunga (North Face, first ascent, 1980), Annapurna I (winter solo attempt, 1981), K2 (leader, summit climber, 1982 Japanese North Ridge team), Scotland ice climbs (1983), Ama Dablam (1985, solo)

In describing Naoe Sakashita, Yvon Chouinard once said, "He climbs like a Japanese samurai."

In fact, Sakashita, who translated Chouinard's book *Climbing Ice* into Japanese, comes from a samurai family. He explained, "Three or four hundred years ago, the samurai had a very difficult life. They had to fight many people to practice their sword techniques. It was dangerous, but it made them have a strong confidence. I have tried to develop this same confidence in my climbing.

"I started my climbing when I was nineteen years old. At that time, I was a student, and there were many reasons why the students were protesting the government. At first, I protested against the government and demonstrated against the college. My partner and I and one or two friends joined about 95 percent of the students to protest against the government. After a year, they returned to study. Otherwise they would have lost their grades. I had no interest in going to the university any more, because many of my friends had stopped protesting. I didn't go to the university for three or four months, and one of my close friends said, 'You should do something, otherwise you will be spoiled,' and he took me to the mountain. After that I found my ability, or my fitness for the mountain, and I continued climbing from that time.

"At first, I climbed the domestic mountains a lot. After that it seemed the natural way to go higher, more difficult, tougher. There are many mountains in the Himalayas I want to climb, because they are very near Japan. Next year I will go to Cho Oyu, myself and one other. Before Cho Oyu, I will attempt some small difficult mountain."

Through his work in distributing outdoor equipment in Japan, Sakashita has made many friends in America. This has given him an insight into the American people. He compared their attitudes with those of the Japanese people.

"I realize that American people and Japanese people are different. They have different ideas about danger. Japanese rock is very loose and our weather is very bad, so these conditions are normal for Japanese people. But in the U.S., American people climb on very stable rock, but [they climb] very difficult mountains, difficult routes, like Yosemite or in the Tetons, and maybe American people are scared of loose rock and bad weather.

"The Japanese climber is underated. British climbers and American climbers are evaluated by many people, as are French and Germans. I think the Japanese did the most splendid climbing in the Himalayan mountains. I have many friends who can climb, and I can compare with others all over the world. Maybe Polish, Czech, and Yugoslavian climbers are underrated, too.

"I think mountaineering or climbing is a dangerous sport, but it is not the only one. For example, a motor bike is a very dangerous thing to drive. Many young kids have been killed by a motor bike, but many people still ride them. They know how dangerous this is, so they accept the danger, but they get something with the danger, something like speed, excitement, relaxation. It is the same in the mountains. In my case, I find many things in the mountains that I couldn't if I stayed in a town or city. But in the mountains, of course, there are many dangerous places. Under the dangerous conditions, I found something. I found myself under the severe conditions. I also found many ideas, many reasons why I will go to climb. I live in the central part of Tokyo where it is the most crowded. We can get any food, we can get any entertainment. In the past, human beings and animals were seeking only some food, warmth, a peaceful place—but now it has changed. Now men want to just relax in their homes, take some good food, watch TV, and go to a warm bed. This is completely different from man's origin.

"I think I have a kind of nostalgia for the primitive life in my heart—very deep in my heart. For example, on Ama Dablam, it was four days of continuous climbing with very little food the last two days—only two Top Raman noodles for two days. I had no sleeping bag, no comfortable tent, no down gear. I just built my camp on my ropes with some small sleeping cover.

"I had confidence that I would live under those conditions, because I was still alive after the K2 bivouac at 8,300 meters. Ama Dablam is only 6,800 meters, so that was no problem for me, but still I was very cold, very hungry, but maybe, I think, enjoying it a little bit. I didn't take any sleeping bag or bivouac gear because I know I can live. It's a simple reason. I didn't want to carry a heavy bag. Maybe it's one experience to help me do more high mountains."

Perhaps it is his past success on mountains; perhaps it is his samurai heritage. But when Naoe Sakashita faces difficulties on a mountain, he becomes determined.

"I want to reach the summit," he explained. "I think I am a dangerous person. When I climbed K2, I didn't consider anything except reaching the summit. It was a crazy thing, but many people do that. For example, if you fall in love with some beautiful girl, you will do anything. If you are a very stable man, you will consider everything about her job, her family, her money, her future—but a normal person doesn't consider all of that. He just says, 'I love you.' That's all. Before falling in love he may consider other things, but after falling in love he doesn't consider very much. The summit for me is the same thing."

Sakashita compared himself to a musician or an artist who becomes obsessed with his work, so obsessed that those outside might consider him crazy in his passion, but who, in his own mind, has weighed the choices and balanced the scales.

"Many of my friends have been killed in the mountains. On the K2 expedition, a member of the expedition was killed. Many famous climbers get killed, like Joe Tasker, Peter Boardman. I remember Annapurna I, first ascent, a French ascent. Maybe half of them have been killed on mountains. Also, Annapurna I South Face, a Bonington team, maybe 40 percent of them killed on mountains. Dougal Haston, Mick Burke. I think most climbers believe, 'That won't happen to me.' I used to believe this, but now I don't think so. The Annapurna I winter expedition was very dangerous for me. Climbing in the Himalayan Mountains is really dangerous. So maybe in the future I will die if I continue to climb. I realize this now. I will continue to go. I think—my life is just one time. I won't have a second time or third time so I wish to live as I like. My hobby is climbing. I did many kind of sports, but climbing is best for me. I realize myself. I enjoy it. I have traveled to many countries. I meet many foreigners. I have many friends, like Yvon [Chouinard]. If I didn't climb, I wouldn't have any chance to go to the U.S., or to Nepal, or Afghanistan, or Russia, or China, or anywhere. Maybe I would work in Tokyo like a common Japanese person from nine to five. Many climbers want to be unique or special. Maybe I can express myself through climbing. I am different from any other person."

Jeff Lowe

Born:
September 13, 1950, Ogden, Utah
Hometown:
Lyons, Colorado
Occupation:
Design and promotion consultant
Climbing Highlights:
Grand Central Couloir on Mt. Kichener (first ascent), Stewart
Falls in Utah (first ascent), Keystone Green Steps in Alaska (first
ascent), North Face of Kwangde in Nepal (first ascent), North
Face of Angel's Landing, West Buttress of Square Top, Bridalveil
Falls (first ascent and solo ascent), South East Pillar of Pumori
(winter solo), South Face of Ama Dablam (solo first ascent), East
Face of Taweche (first ascent, winter), walls in Zion and
Yosemite. More than 700 first ascents of rock climbing routes
and more than 4,000 total climbs

In 1974, Jeff Lowe gained attention for the first ascent of Bridalveil Falls. His name became associated with ice climbing and, in 1979, with the publication of his book, *The Ice Experience*, a cover story in *Sports Illustrated*, and appearances on *Merv Griffin* and *Good Morning America*, his reputation as a master ice climber was firmly established.

That reputation, Lowe said, might be a little misleading. "Most of the public perception of my climbing comes through articles and information about ice because it was unusual when I started to climb ice, but I've done far more rock climbing than ice climbing. I still maintain more of an interest in rock climbing, although I like ice climbing. I like it all. Rock climbing—free climbing—is real climbing to me. It always has been. For every first ascent on a waterfall, I've probably done twenty first ascents on rock."

Lowe has been climbing for thirty years. "I've been climbing so long that I don't remember what life was like without climbing. It's the same with skiing. I've climbed and skied since I was barely old enough to remember. I didn't consciously choose to take up climbing or skiing, and to me they're the same, by the way. The motivations and the things they satisfy for me are really similar. They started about the same time in my life and I've always continued them. I was too young to really know that there was a choice to climb or ski. I just started climbing and skiing, and I enjoyed the feelings that I got from climbing and skiing. I don't think

I ever went through that period of questioning why they climb that most climbers do who start at a later date. It was all so natural to me that I didn't even question it.

"I think it suits me really well physiologically. I feel really comfortable in the mountains, and I think it suits me temperamentally, too, to be on my own a lot. I like people, but I like to be alone as well. That's just a temperamental thing. I'm really addicted to the perspective that I get when I'm away from society and in the mountains and dealing with something that's real on a different level than society is real. When you are up in the mountains and you look down, even the most majestic city looks pretty small; civilization really is shown up for what it is, which is really kind of insignificant in the overall scheme of things. I like that reminder of the unimportance of man, really, to anybody or anything else. The only importance that we have is to ourselves, and so we have created our own sense of self-importance and there we are. But getting away from that in the mountains, where you realize that your life or death is totally insignificant, and looking down, where the greatest constructions of mankind are really nothing in any real sense of the word, just gives me a great feeling for the vastness of things and for the reality which is greater than human concerns. I think the point that I'm trying to make is that it has lent a perspective to my life that is a little unique and doesn't follow along with the belief that mankind is that important. I really don't think that we are, and that gives me a way of accepting things that I don't think I'd have if I really believed that everything that I did was important and that everything that everybody else did was important in a serious sense of the word. It's all kind of—not a joke—but it's possible to live life on the lighter side.

"Physically, I feel that climbing is the finest form of all-around exercise that there is. I've tried a lot of other sports, but they just don't give you the overall workout and feeling of mind integrated into body that climbing does. The dynamics of interaction of mind and body in all types, and in an infinite variety, of positions and situations is really what keeps it interesting year after year.

"You do a route and give it a name and if people like it and talk about it, that's real satisfying to be a part of this ongoing evolutionary development of human experience in a way that positively affects other people. Then to have feedback from other people regarding your contribution is real interesting.

"Then, there's the adventure side of it, too. The foreign trips are all a part of climbing. It's kind of been an excuse to travel, and you don't feel just like a tourist because you've got a purpose for being there. You know, I'm going to Asia to climb or I'm going to Peru to climb when, in reality, the climbing is only part of it and, in fact, maybe not the most important part."

Lowe's father was the one who first introduced him to climbing. "He loved going to the Tetons whenever he got the chance and he was friends with the guides there. He gave all his kids an opportunity to try climbing at a young age. He had eight kids and three of us kind of liked it and stayed with it—Mike, Greg, and myself. In 1956, when I was six years old, I started climbing, and I climbed every summer as a teenager in the Tetons, in Little Cottonwood Canyon, and all over northern Utah during the sixties and also down in Yosemite towards the latter part of that decade."

In thinking back on his climbs, he reflects, "I like long free climbs like Black Elk in the Wind Rivers. That's a Grade V free climb. My best free climbs have combined challenging difficulty with long runouts like Seamstress Corner near Telluride, which is six pitches of 5.10 to 5.11 + climbing with long runouts and sparse protection. I liked New Music on Lumpy Ridge which has thirty-foot runouts on 5.11, and Risky Business on the Northeast Face of Chief's Head which has really long runouts on 5.10 and some longish runouts on 5.11 and 5.11 +."

Then there was the North Face of Kwangde in Nepal. It was a unique ascent and gave Lowe the "best ice climb I've done and probably one of the most challenging ice climbs in the world. At least it's in a class with very few others. It is seasonal ice on that type of mountain and is only there about a month out of the year. It consists of compact granite slabs overlain by thin—not water ice—but extremely hard, porcelain-like snow frozen to these really steep granite slabs. It's an El Capitan-type ice climb with very little protection. We did some 500-foot pitches by tying two 100-meter ropes together to get to the belays, so it's a totally different type of climb. It combines waterfall ice climbing difficulties with the seriousness of a Himalayan climb, and it has to be done in winter because that is the only time it exists. It ties all the elements together in terms of ice climbing. No one had been seriously looking at these smears of ice on the big Himalayan walls in winter yet. It may be the first and only climb of its sort. It was totally fun.

"One of the best free climbs I've done was in Peru, on the North Buttress of Puscanturpa Norte, which I soloed in 1983 and made the first free ascent. It had been climbed once before by an Italian expedition, which spent about ten days on the thing and did a lot of aid [direct aid climbing]. I soloed it in six hours at about 5.10. That's my best long, solo free climb."

For Lowe, making a successful climb alone is a special experience. "I like it a lot, but I try not to do it very much unless I just can't stop myself. Sometimes I feel safer on my own than with a partner. I feel like I can move more quickly, more efficiently, and often times that translates to greater speed and therefore greater safety. Of course, if something does go wrong, you are more exposed. It's like cheating to do that because it's all so easy compared to going with a partner or an expedition, and it all happens so much more quickly. When you can climb up a wall in ten hours that would take an expedition a week even alpine style, it feels like cheating. It's seductive that way and that's why I say I try not to do too much of it. It feels too good.

"I have dreams and I have visions. I've been following one kind of vision for a number of years. For about fifteen years, I've had a vision of doing the hardest and most attractive faces in the Himalayas in alpine style or solo and even in the winter. I've only partially realized that dream and there's still another step or two to take, going to some higher peaks or harder faces. A climb I just completed with John Roskelley, the East Face of Taweche, is a step along this road.

"There are two climbs that come close to my idea of the best there is and one of them is Latok. We were on the North Ridge of Latok in 1978 and failed, but we got really close. That was close to an ultimate climb for me. Then, I've had two failures on the South Pillar of Nuptse, which is at a higher elevation and on a large scale, with real technical climbing. It's on a level of difficulty that you won't find on many mountains that high. Now it seems more realistic than it did ten years ago to consider doing that, but it has yet to be accomplished."

Even after so many years in climbing, Lowe is still taking part in the changes and developments of the sport. He organized the first international artificial wall climbing competition held in the United States at Snow Bird in Utah. Before he got involved, however, he had to have a change of heart.

"Being a traditionalist, I was against competition to start with, but mainly I was against the destruction of the cliffs and the environment, like all the bolts next to good routes on the cliffs. When you put them on an artificial wall, it removes that environmental concern and suddenly you can watch a really beautiful and intense form of gymnastics. The level of climbing that [the artificial wall] is inspiring is far beyond what would have happened without it. This is just coming to this country and it's going to change the level at which everybody climbs. For me personally, that means that I'll be able to go to the Himalayas and have a better chance of doing some of the things that I want to do in free climbing. My feeling is that even an old guy like me can go out and climb 5.13 if I train and work on these walls. That means that in the Himalayas you can maybe climb an easy 5.12 with some degree of expediency. That opens up a lot more of the terrain on the big walls to free climbing."

Opening up terrain on big walls is just what Lowe wants to do. On an expedition in the Himalayas, he saw a peak called the Grand Cathedral, which had a massive rock face with two parallel cracks running from bottom to top. He knew immediately that he wanted to climb it.

"The peak is under 20,000 feet—about 19,500—but the wall is 5,000 feet from glacier to summit and will be the biggest free climb in the world if we can do it, and at a high elevation. There is going to be a lot of hard climbing, but the rock there lends itself to free climbing. It's the next thing that inspires me to upgrade my free climbing to another level so I can go.

"The idea is to try a completely free climb. If we use one point of aid it will be a failure. I think because of the crack systems, we'll be able to do it, but it will require the team to be climbing at a really high standard. It's the kind of thing that keeps me going. Other expeditions are going over there and nailing up the things. That doesn't interest me at all. There are a few climbs of some of the big walls over there every year, but no one seems to be dedicating their energy to completely free climbing them. That's what really interests me now."

Jim Bridwell

Born:
July 29, 1944, San Antonio, Texas

Hometown:
Palm Desert, California

Occupation:
Climbing guide, photojournalist

Climbing Highlights:
Yosemite climbs, including Pacific Ocean Wall, Sea of Dreams, Aquarium, Free Stone on Geek Tower, Northwest Face of Half Dome (two new routes), Nabisco Wall, Hot Line on Elephant Rock, Final Exam on Half Dome, Mt. Watkins (new route). Many climbs in Patagonia, including Cerro Torre (first ascent), and Alaskan climbs including the East Face of Moose's Tooth

"Climbing was something I sort of fell into," explained Jim Bridwell. "Like Yvon [Chouinard], strangely enough, I used to catch birds of prey to train them for falconry. I just wanted to know how to get to the bird nests that were on the cliffs.

"In grade school I played basketball and other team sports. Then I moved to California and it seemed that the coach always had his team picked, so I went into track, because there was no judgment to be made. The guy who is fastest is fastest. The guy who jumps highest jumps highest.

"Climbing was something to fulfill that athletic desire. It was away from the mainstream and wasn't influenced by outside attitudes, so it was something that I liked, and I fit in right away. My father was in the military and we traveled around a lot. It was hard for me to fit in socially because [as a military child] you are ripped out of one place and put in another, and you meet a few kids and have to prove yourself. I think when you are young you are delicate when you don't fit in, so you hold back a little bit from society or people."

Bridwell has had a long career as a leading force in the development of climbing. In fact, John Roskelley called him the "grandfather of American rock climbing." His reputation, like that of most climbers, has been limited to notoriety within the climbing community.

"In the United States, I see myself as sort of an unofficial athlete. If I were in Europe, I might be more like a Reggie Jackson—maybe not that much—but I would be an athlete. I don't think climbing is something Americans even think about. If they do think about it, they think it is strange. One time I heard a lady and a man talking about climbers on El Cap and she said, 'There ought to be a law against that.' That's exactly what she said. It is something that is so adverse to the parental attitudes of most Americans. You know, you don't have a right to choose what you do. They're always trying to protect you. I think you have a right to choose your own way of learning.

"Geographically, the United States is a large area and most of it doesn't have any mountains. Naturally, climbing is mainly located where the mountains are. You don't turn on the TV on Sunday afternoon and see climbing. Like soccer, it's catching on here, but it's slow. So Americans just aren't educated as far as unusual sports go.

"Most of the sports that people like in America are directly competitive against another person. That is a very difficult thing to judge in climbing. Somebody might ask, 'Who is the best climber?' There is no best climber. You can't get that cut and dried comparison. Also, most American sports [center on] hand/eye coordination and their attitudes are in that direction. Whereas in Europe, you have alpine countries where everything is mountains. You get a ride with somebody over there and they will ask you a question like, 'Are you a free-climber?' Here most people don't know what that means."

One thing that has helped to bring climbing out into the open is the number of books and magazines about climbing that have been published in recent years.

Bridwell remembered, "When I started climbing it was taboo to talk about, or publicize, climbing. Climbers tried to keep it away from the masses. There was an aloof type of attitude towards climbing. It had nothing to do with the masses. Then suddenly, younger climbers came along and tried to make a buck off it and make themselves famous. After climbing for ten or fifteen years, I was still poor as ever and some of the other guys were making money. It bothered me because I didn't know for sure what to do. Making the money would make it easier to live, but I had grown up with this tradition. I wish I could say, 'It's been velly, velly good to me,' but I can't." He joked.

"If I had been in Europe, I would have been able to make a good living off climbing. I might not have been as good because the situation in Yosemite was conducive to climbing every day; never bad weather. You could train, and I was there at the perfect time. There were many new routes to do.

"A lot of us became famous without even knowing it, because there started to be literature, climbing magazines. When I started there was the *Sierra Club Bulletin*, but no *Mountain* magazine or *Climbing* magazine. It wasn't a well-publicized sport or activity. It sort of hid from the rest of the world.

"The first time I ever knew that anybody even paid attention to me was when I went into a restaurant in Yosemite and I heard some young climber say, 'That's Jim Bridwell,' and it was because of the magazines. It felt weird. It was something I didn't understand. It made me feel uncomfortable because I was in the public eye. [It was] a small spectrum of the public, but nonetheless, I wasn't used to the attention."

Climbing is not just a physical activity for Bridwell. It has often been a form of expression.

"I always just wanted to create my own art form. I just did climbs that I wanted to do, mainly focusing on first ascents. I've always felt I wanted to add something to climbing. Like Kim [Schmitz] and I—if we did an existing route on El Cap, we wanted to do it in a substantially faster time, or use substantially more free climbing on it. We wanted to be in the vanguard of what was happening or at least be expressive of our own creative attitudes.

"I think climbing is an art form. It is like gymnastics, dancing, painting—you have the rock as a canvas and you express your idea in the route. That's been my attitude towards climbing. It's a chance to do something new and creative and beautiful. If it is clean, beautiful rock and a line that stands out as pure—good, consistent, hard climbing all the way, good quality moves, consistent in its nature and texture—then it has something to say."

Over the years, Bridwell has been able to make significant statements through his routes, many of which have been called visionary like the Aquarium Wall, which, as Bridwell explained, "involved putting together small features that don't jump out at you, [which are] more subtle. That hadn't been done yet. People picked out the natural, big cracks, giant corners, and the cracks didn't vary much. We decided to put together little things to make an entire route. That was one of the first climbs of that nature."

Another climb that was especially important to Bridwell was the Pacific Ocean Wall. "I think it was a big breakthrough, both for artificial climbing and for myself. I used to feel nervous and uptight about doing a big wall. After the Pacific Ocean Wall, nothing bothered me. If I could do that, there could be nothing worse.

"One summer I did three of the best routes I've ever done. The first was called the Sea of Dreams. At that time, Pacific Ocean was the hardest technical route in the world. Then we went and did the Sea of Dreams, which was quite a bit harder. Then we did a new route on Half Dome. It's a beautiful route. We did another route on Watkins, named after a friend of mine who died on Watkins. These are all state-of-the-art artificial routes."

Because he lacked the money to travel extensively, Bridwell spent several years climbing in Yosemite. This helped him be more influential in climbing there, but caused him to get a reputation as only a rock climber. He wanted to try alpine climbing, but didn't have the contacts to get on an expedition. After reading an article by Italian climber Cesare Maestri about an early attempt on Cerro Torre, Bridwell saved his money and headed for Patagonia.

"I read the article and I said, 'That is the epitome of climbing.' I went down a couple of years later and did Cerro Torre in my own inimitable style. I picked up this guy who had hitchhiked into the area and we did it. The first almost-ascent by Maestri took over fifty days. We ended up finishing the ascent for him [Maestri], for us. It was sort of a mutual ascent.

"We did bring a new attitude to it, weaning ourselves from the fixed rope and just going for it. That was satisfying. We hiked by the Italians on our way up and they saw our light on Cerro Torre and thought it was a star. We were very lucky. We had good weather. It was ideal, which is not usual.

"Then I did a new route on Kichatna Spire, which had only been climbed once before and had been attempted by some noted climbers, Royal Robbins and others. Once again we had ideal weather."

In Europe, Bridwell ran into problems on a route called the Shroud. "I got hit in the mouth by a rock. It was down low on the climb and the rock knocked a couple of teeth loose. We continued on and made a successful ascent. We had a forced bivouac, and I had these teeth wiggling around in my mouth all night. I had a big hole in my lip—not very comfortable. We came down the next day, and I was starving. The guy I was with ordered a big meal and I couldn't eat with these loose teeth, so I just had to go in the bathroom and rip them out with my fingers so I could eat. Then I took a nail file and filed off the sharp points."

Perhaps his statements on rock were a warm-up for another creation. "I've been contemplating writing a book. It's an autobiography, but it's pretty hard to talk about yourself. I think I have an idea of how I want to approach it. It wouldn't necessarily be about me, which I think would be pretentious, but it would be about friends. One person I would write about is Layton Kor, who laid down much of the groundwork for climbing in Yosemite. My kid's name is Layton, after him, and he was one of the people who really had a lot to do with my interest in climbing. One of the things that Kor really impressed me with was his mixed climbing, going off of hard aid into hard free climbing with a clarity that you don't see these days because people are more focused on one or the other style. You don't see that type of broad development. He was one of the masters.

"Kor was always full of energy. People used to say, 'Kor is coming, we'd better hide, because he'll want to do everything.' He would do one first ascent after another. He was funny, too. I remember one time we were coming down and he said, 'When we get down, the locals will be trying to give us their daughters.' "

Climbing is the way Bridwell has lived his entire adult life. "It's not something that I question. You might ask the questions, Why is there life? Is there a God? If there is a God, why would He want to create man? Or did He? I think anything that you put your life's energy into becomes part of your identity; to lose that is to lose part of yourself or what you have created. You perpetuate the image. Good or bad, you're stuck with it. It's something that you do that you identify with your personality. It would be difficult for the Rolling Stones to not play rock and roll anymore, because that's their image of themselves. When you've convinced everybody that that's who you are, that's who you are.

"Don't get me wrong. I don't think climbing is important at all." He laughed. "You need a way to express yourself, something creative. You can draw or be a painter or a surgeon, but you need something to put your energies into, otherwise they spoil inside you and you sour. In terms of the universe, climbing has very little to do with anything. I think it's all a part of the art of life, understanding how all that stuff out there fits together and how you can apply it to your life."

Royal Robbins

Born:

February 3, 1935, Point Pleasant, West Virginia

Hometown:

Modesto, California

Occupation:

Owner, outdoor clothing and
equipment business

Climbing Highlights:

Several major routes on El Capitan including the West Face (first ascent), Salathe Wall (first ascent), North American Wall (first ascent), Dihedral Wall (second ascent), Muir Wall (second ascent, solo), Nose (second ascent, first continuous ascent); other Yosemite routes on Half Dome (first ascent of North West Face), Leaning Tower (solo), Sentinal (solo of Steck-Salathe), and many new routes on Taquitz Rock. Routes in the Alps including West Face Direct of the Dru (first ascent), and climbs in the Dolomites, Mt. Proboscis, Canada, (first ascent, South East Face). More than two dozen kayaking first descents of rivers

Perhaps no one else in the history of climbing has inspired as many would-be climbers to go out for the first time as Royal Robbins. His own outstanding climbing achievements motivated some, but even more were moved by his two books, *Basic Rockcraft* and *Advanced Rockcraft*. These books became the basic texts for two decades of climbers who began during the years when climbing matured as a sport.

"This gives me a sense of wonder," Robbins said. "When I started climbing I read books and I pictured climbing a peak. I heard about people who stood up in front of audiences and told about their climbs. It never remotely occurred to me when I started climbing that I would be doing any of those things. It seemed like such a rarified activity. Much less did I ever think that I would become famous in the small way that climbers are. It's very gratifying. It's nice to have respect. I'd like to think that I've largely earned it, but I think that I ended up getting more than I deserved."

His climbing and his books got Robbins started. Then he tried entering the business world by opening a climbing-shoe shop in a basement in Modesto. He continually added more products and improved his business until he was able to move out on his own. The business, operated with his wife Liz, was called Mountain

Paraphernalia. Later they changed the name to Robbins Mountain Gear, and then simply to Royal Robbins.

From its early beginnings in the basement shop, the business, which in time included Robbins's own line of outdoor apparel, expanded to more than forty employees and a multimillion dollar annual volume. Robbins is quick to see the connection between success on a rock face and success in a business.

"In terms of a common thread, it is mainly tenacity that helps you operate closer to your maximum—tenacity of purpose regardless of your talents or intelligence or a lot of other things. You can make up for almost anything if you are steadfast and keep going in a certain direction steadily for a long time.

"It is important to succeed in what you start out attempting, so if you are attempting something difficult, then by the very nature of it, you have to feel good when you achieve it. It's kind of a built-in reward. To get the reward, you have to keep going.

"I'm tenacious and I'm competitive, mostly with myself. I'm not perfect. I think one likes to get appreciation and respect from one's peers, and that was important to me. Rarely does one climb in a vacuum totally, solely for oneself. There is the desire to be respected and to let other people know what you've done. The worst part of competition is when you talk down other climbers, or say something to detract from their accomplishments. Most of us have done that at one time or another. Whenever I've done it, I regret having done it. The essense of the competition is to judge yourself, not others."

Although by most people's standards, Robbins has been successful in several arenas, he doesn't quite see it that way. "The funny thing is that I haven't succeeded in what I attempted in climbing. I have gotten greater successes in what I attempted, in a sense, but I haven't succeeded in becoming as good a climber as I wanted to be, just in terms of ability, so you couldn't say I've succeeded in that area. Success is a question of where you set your goals.

"I may have reached my potential, but that is not the same thing as saying I achieved what I wanted to achieve. I know there were always a lot of climbers around who were better than I was. There are a lot of better ones now. People have done things I couldn't even imagine doing. My ambition was to become the best climber and I never did. I think that goal was the wrong goal. It's a goal that sets you up for disappointment, obviously. I don't have that goal anymore. I have a broader picture now. It was kind of a narrow view, but it was useful for motivating me strongly, for getting myself to work hard. I think a better goal is to put more emphasis on enjoyment and on getting a rounded experience and on things like friendship, rather than on sheer achievement."

By setting his goals so high, Robbins put himself in a position where he was a major factor in determining the directions a young, developing sport would take. This often led to disagreements with other climbers over what types of equipment or what methods of ascent should be used in establishing new routes.

Robbins and his partners had made several routes on El Capitan in Yosemite. That group felt that drilling bolts into the rock should be kept to a bare minimum, if done at all. Another group of climbers, which included Warren Harding, did not feel the same way. In 1970, Harding and Dean Caldwell made a first ascent called the Wall of the Early Morning Light or the Dawn Wall. They used some three hundred bolts during the twenty-six-day climb. Not long after, Robbins and Don Lauria, thinking such extensive use of bolts would devalue other routes on El Capitan, set out to climb the route and chopped the bolts off the early pitches. They later changed their minds and finished the route, leaving the bolts on the upper route.

In retrospect, Robbins said, "I shouldn't have chopped Harding's bolts on the Dawn Wall. It was a mistake. I was thinking wrong. It was something we stopped after we started and was something that shouldn't have been started in the first place. I was basically acting out, on an action level, a philosophical kind of debate that people with Warren's philosophy were stating one way and people of mine were stating another. I think we should have left it purely to the words and left the action out."

Robbins felt badly about his move against Harding's route, but, once again, he had a strong influence on how the sport was progressing. Many years later, the use of bolts and other ethical issues are still the subject of campfire talk at climbing areas throughout the world.

In recent years, Robbins has slowed down his climbing and is spending more time guiding his kayak down uncharted rivers. He enjoys the thrill of the white-water. "There is much area there for doing firsts without having an enormous amount of skills. It's a bit like Yosemite was when we were climbing there in the sixties. There were a lot of first ascents to be done and you didn't have to have the skill that's needed these days to do important first ascents in Yosemite. We didn't have to train the way people train today, and we could still have super adventures. Kayaking and river running in the United States is a little like that now. It's good adventure and exciting. We can do a first. There are a lot of them left to be done and it's a little bit easier on the body. If I didn't have kayaking, I'd be climbing a lot more now. It's just that you can't do both, and while there's a lot of interesting kayaking to be done, I'm putting more of my time in on that."

Climbing was his first interest, however. "I think most of us who are climbers recognize that we have a deep-seated need for some sort of battle as part of our lives. I used to like getting up in the mountains and hiking around, but I knew I wanted something more exciting. I've said much more than that in the past, but I've come to see that it's that simple.

"Certainly there's something in climbing that fulfills a deep need. Otherwise climbers wouldn't be so passionate about what they do. You can start off with the premise that, whatever that need is, it is being filled. It may be very different things for different people, but it is something real and strong. It's almost putting too much on it to say that maybe we all climb for reasons that we can't admit. Maybe the reason that the question is so difficult to answer is that the truth is unfaceable. Maybe that's why we stumble.

"At this point, in looking back, I think one of the key things to remember for young climbers aspiring to do well is don't take yourself too seriously. Don't have a fixed idea in mind of what you are going to accomplish, because you may or may not accomplish it. The important thing is to concentrate on doing the best you can rather than on what you are trying to achieve. Your achievements tend to come much more fruitfully when you are not thinking about them, when you are thinking about what you are doing at the moment and doing it as well as you can."

Beverly Johnson

Born:

April 22, 1947, Annapolis, Maryland

Hometown:

Los Angeles, California and Kelly, Wyoming

Occupation:

Filmmaker

Climbing Highlights:

Shawangunks, Yosemite climbs including El Capitan (first all-woman team and first female solo), Sentinel, Leaning Tower (solo), and many others. Filming trips to Antarctica, Afghanistan, and the North Pole

"The thing that I enjoy about climbing is watching other people climb and how they approach the same problem, particularly on a route that's pretty much within everybody's limit," expressed Beverly Johnson. "If three or four of you are climbing together and pushing it, not something that you can do casually, there are many different ways to do the same thing. And they all work. Some will work for some people and not for others because of body size or balance. If you climb places like the Shawangunks there are endless possibilities.

"I like straightforward cracks. I like moving. I don't like standing still for long periods of time. Crack climbing is kind of that way. You've got to move or fall out. The real art in climbing, as everyone will tell you, is being able to rest. You know, he that rests best, climbs the hardest."

Johnson became interested in climbing when she was studying geology in school and went out on field studies. "If I was going out to look at some geology, I'd walk up to the top just to see what was on the other side. After a while, the climbing got to be more interesting than the geology or the view. It does command your attention when you get yourself stuck. Suddenly the view doesn't matter. And you couldn't care less about the geology as long as you aren't falling on any of it. So your interest is focused by necessity."

One person in particular motivated Johnson to try harder routes and improve her climbing. "[Royal] Robbins would come up and make these absolute flat statements about what no woman could do. After Elaine Matthews did the West Face of Sentinel, Robbins heard about it and, in my presence, said, 'Well, it will be a long time before a woman does the Steck-Salethe [route on the Sentinel].' The next morning I was up there, but it had never crossed my mind to do it before Robbins suggested it in his off-handed, sneaky way, which I'm sure he was contriving all along. After you know Robbins a little bit, he's like that.

"People get you going in that way. Just asking questions and hearing what people recommend focuses your direction. I asked [Chuck] Pratt, when I began in Yosemite, for some route recommendations and what he recommended determined a lot of what I wanted to do.

"I climbed with men a lot, and I sort of developed this attitude that women were incompetent, myself included. It kind of becomes self-fulfilling. You know, 'Girls can't do that.' I've found that climbing with other women was really fun, much more fun than climbing with men, because you've got the same sort of giggles. 'Look what us girls did today.' But on some more serious routes it was a problem, because it was hard for the other women. You expect them to be like a guy, but they're not. Maybe that's an old-fashioned attitude, but it was what I was raised with.

"I used to work on a fire crew. If somebody gave me a bunch of people and I was going to pick a fire crew out of this bunch of people, I'd pick the big guys first. All other things being equal, you know they're going to be stronger and they're more likely to have shovel experience. How many woman really use a hammer? The answer is more and more, but the men will probably have more experience.

"This isn't to say that women can't do the really hard routes in the mountains, but they're going to do it differently. They're not going to meet everything head on with the same bullheadedness. I would encourage that, too—that women view the problem with their strengths and not try to be like men."

Much of the attention Beverly Johnson received from the climbing world was for her long solo routes. "The thing that is nice about solo climbing—and you don't realize it until you do it—is that there has always been somebody at the other end of the rope and now, when there isn't anybody, it's like one whole antagonism is gone. You miss a lot of the neat parts of climbing when you do it by yourself, because you see all these neat things that you need to share to make it real. If it's just for yourself, it maybe doesn't register as it should. You lose that, but you also gain. It is tremendously peaceful.

"When I soloed the Leaning Tower, one day I just sat in my hammock and read. I love to read. It was nice and I didn't feel like going anywhere. I was drying my sleeping bag, so I hung it out and laid in the sun. When you've got a partner, even if they agree to stay there, you're thinking in the back of your mind. 'Are they liking this or are they not liking this?' And they're telling you old war stories or you're telling them old war stories, which is even worse, and it just isn't the same.

"I have to rate the Leaning Tower as the most fun thing I've ever done climbing. There were two things. I had never done the route before, so I don't really know this, but I'm convinced that solo is the only way you should do it, because if you do it with a partner, you don't get to rappel and it's got the nicest rappels in the world. It's all aid. Soloing free climbing is really hard. On the Leaning Tower you don't have to muck around with that. You just slide the prusik up and however long you take is okay. Nobody's got a watch, you're not worried about anything. What I did that was kind of fun was I presumed that if you pulled the rope up and left a little slack, you could rappel right into your anchors, even though each pitch was forty feet overhanging. I would just clip in, push off, let go and go right into space. I'd put my feet out and stop right on a dime. It was perfect. Then I would jug up and clean the pitch, haul the bag, no big deal. It was a better experience to solo than to do it with somebody. On most of the climbs that you do by yourself, however, you dread hauling the bag and that kind of thing."

In addition to hanging on vertical rock walls for days by herself, Johnson has found other ways of adding excitement to her life.

"I was down in South America with a folding kayak and I put it in a river about which I had obtained only the vaguest local description—in Spanish, which I don't speak—and information that there were *saltos* [waterfalls] fifty meters high. I had a one million to one aircraft sectional map and it was a big adventure. It's not foolish. What I consider foolishness is when you go into uncertainty with no plan for getting yourself out of it. What I did in South America was to say, 'Okay, I'm going to go down here and make some calculated chances that there's nothing totally blind that I'm going to hit, but I'm also going to be aware that the bottom line is that I'll leave the Klepper [kayak] and hike back out and I'm not going to worry about it. There's an exit for you and you've got enough stuff.' That turned out to be no problem, despite the local description. The best part of that was just putting the boat in and sensing the unknown, as much as things can be unknown in modern times when satellites photograph every inch of the earth."

She also walked to the North Pole as part of a film crew documenting the Transglobe Expedition organized by Sir Ranulph Fiennes. "The nicest part was walking across Ellesmere Island," she recalled. "It's just beautiful. We went up in the spring to Alert. We started out on snowmobiles and went about 150 miles to Cape Columbia. As soon as we got on the sea ice there was no way we could make it on snowmobiles, so we pulled sleds for the next month. We started the thirteenth of February and got to the Pole on the tenth of April.

"People get involved in risk sports for many reasons. I remember one time I went out when I had this description that said to go up here and traverse here and climb up to this bolt. I came to where the bolt was supposed to be and somebody had chopped it. My legs started shaking, and this was the first time I had had that experience of thinking, 'Oh, now I'm going to die,' because from there I would have hit the ground in a fall. I was sixty or seventy feet out and thought, 'What am I going to do?' All of a sudden, it's like you can turn a whole set off in your mind and your legs stop shaking, there's no more ground, there's only this little square of the problem in front of your face, and it's only exactly as wide as what you can deal with at that moment. I don't really remember the circumstances, but I do remember standing there and going from being panicked to being very cool. Both feet were slipping. One foot would slip and then the other foot would slip and I just kept replacing them while I thought about what to do. There was no hurry about it. I ended up making this nice little move and an elegant traverse off the route and the end of that was so satisfying. It's not a situation you would put yourself into, but it's just a situation that you sometimes meet.

"It's like standing on the edge and having to control these factors which have a very critical outcome. If there's a big net down there, it just isn't the same. You don't want to get in that situation, but when you see the monster coming up, you deal with it. If we all lived forever, I don't know that people would bother going climbing. Think of climbing if you had wings. How interesting would that be?"

Galen Rowell

Born:
August 23, 1940, Berkeley, California
Hometown:
Berkeley, California
Occupation:
Photographer, writer
Climbing Highlights:
Everest (1983 West Ridge, climbing leader), K2 (1975,
unsuccessful), McKinley (ski traverse and one-day ascent), Mt.
Dickey (first ascent, South East Face), Lukpilla Brakk (first ascent),
Great Trango Tower (first ascent), Anye Machin, Mustagh Ata,
Half Dome (first ascent of South Face), more than one hundred
new routes in Sierra Nevadas, six trips to China and six trips to
Pakistan, 1980 winter ski traverse of Karakoram range from
Indian border to Hunza

It's hard to open an outdoor magazine without seeing photo credits for Galen
Rowell. His photographs have appeared in *National Geographic, National Geographic Traveler, Outside, Time, GEO, Audubon, Sierra, Sports Illustrated, National Wildlife* and many others. He is able to capture the outdoor experience on
film in a way that most climbers are able to do only in their minds.

It doesn't stop with his photography. He has written nine books about the
mountains including *High and Wild; Mountains of the Middle Kingdom; Mountain
Light; Vertical World of Yosemite; In the Throne Room of the Mountain Gods;
Many People Come Looking, Looking; Alaska: Images of the Country* (with John
McPhee); and *The Art of Adventure*. Most recently, he illustrated John Muir's
Yosemite with his photographs. About the stories in *High and Wild*, Rowell remarked, "Of the climbing stories that have ended up in print, those are the closest
to my heart.

"All writers tend to dip into a reservoir of intense personal experience to
produce a book, whether it's fiction or non-fiction. Passion moves them to write.
Unless you have that passion, you're not going to sit down and go through all
the sacrifices and effort to write a book. Hemingway used his kind of experiences
and Joseph Conrad his to color their fiction with reality. Climbers have a much
deeper range of heavy-duty experiences to draw from than the average person,
and I think that is why so many climbers, like myself, are inspired to write."

Rowell was introduced to the wilderness at a young age when his parents took him on Sierra Club family outings. He remembers being ten years old when "I learned all about rappelling and made several practice climbs. I grew up in Berkeley and there were practice rocks within sight of my parents's house. Pinnacle Rock was one of them. The Sierra Club used to come out and do practice climbs, so I learned the basics there. In the summers I scrambled up Sierra peaks, and when I was sixteen, I walked miles over passes into Yosemite and did my first technical climbing there in 1957."

Although he tried many types of climbing, he soon learned that what he liked best was "remote area technical climbing. I like doing new routes on rock faces in the High Sierra and unclimbed spires in the Himalaya. Those are my favorite memories."

He explained, "I really enjoy doing first ascents where I'm covering new ground and being the first person to figure out a new route. The idea of solving problems in mountaineering, of looking at something from below, figuring out how to do it and then actually doing it really appeals to me. Then again, I also enjoy doing classic routes, too. I wouldn't want to eliminate one over the other.

"The natural world is the closest thing I have to religion. If I look for answers about who I am or my relation to the rest of the world, I look to the natural world. Even when I don't directly ask a question and seek an answer, I often have those questions answered for me by my personal experience. When I go into the mountains, it feels right. I intuitively know my place in the world much better through those experiences. The more intense they are, the better I know myself, and the more I am able to challenge myself.

"I didn't like team sports particularly as I was growing up. I never really knew my own contribution. If my baseball team won, was it because I did well or was it because the eight other guys did well or did six of them do well and three of them screw up? Was I one of those three?" He laughed. "I came not to trust direct feedback other than what came from inside me. In most other ways—the grades you get in school, and the like—we are judged by other people. What really appealed to me about climbing was that the feedback came from the natural world where there wasn't anyone judging me. The natural world gives you tangible answers to how you are doing. There are very few other sports that do that. Climbing wasn't directly competitive when I began. It wasn't racing for time against somebody. I remember when an older man, who thought he wouldn't like rock climbing because of his quiet Buddhist nature, saw bouldering for the first time. He said, 'This is the gentlest form of competition I've ever seen.' That's the kind of thing that still appeals to me."

Rowell talked about some of his favorite climbs—the West Ridge of Everest in 1983 when he was the team's climbing leader, the first ascent of Great Trango Tower in 1977 with Roskelley and Schmitz, and the one-day ascent of Mt. McKinley after a ski circumnavigation of the peak.

He said of the McKinley climb, "The idea of being on a mountain that big, where almost everyone's experience is of moving very slowly with a big pack, and of doing the whole mountain with just a day pack was a very free and wonderful experience. That's kind of what I was after, that joy of moving on a big peak with just a day pack, rather than setting a record."

Although as a photographer he spends most of his time looking for the beauty in the mountains, Rowell knows he can't overlook the danger that exists.

"I'm aware of each situation the way I would be driving in heavy traffic," he explained. "I do something intuitively because it's the right move to make. It's not as if there's some sort of red flag going off in my head. I usually don't spend time worrying once I commit myself to something.

"When I did the traverse of the Karakoram, Kim Schmitz and I had a contest to see who could be the most chicken. Basically it was, 'I'm really scared of going underneath that ice fall. I'm going to go way out on the glacier instead.' Or, 'There's no way I'm going to walk over there unroped, I'm chickenshit.' It was a way to play it safe in the wild mountains. Rather than be macho and go straight ahead, we said, 'Hey, we're going to survive this best if we stay aware of dangers and tune into them.' It allowed us to make moves without our egos interfering. Although I might not have danger in my mind all the time, I certainly don't go walking through the mountains tuning it out. I look at it carefully.

"One example of being chickenshit happened to me recently. I was in Nepal trekking with my wife and her brother. I left them to solo a small peak of 20,500 feet. I was only half an hour above the pass when the incident happened. I left a snow plateau and started up a forty-five-degree slope. It looked funny. I can't tell you why, but something didn't seem right. I decided to traverse over to where the snow merged into ice just ten feet above the bottom. I walked a couple hundred yards over, put my crampons on, went up two steps, jumped to test the slope, and a 700-foot fracture opened up across the slope I was going to go up. A huge slab came down, tons of big blocks. The ten feet of stuff above me buried me up to my waist. It was one of those times when I was glad I was chickenshit."

Rowell credits his good luck and happy experiences in the mountains to "a lot of years of mountaineering with many people who have some good intuitive sense about the mountains. The most valuable thing for me was going out in the early days with people like Fred Beckey and Warren Harding and watching how they dealt with the mountains, seeing how they handled dangers on rock."

One of the most dangerous situations Rowell faced was with Warren Harding on the first ascent of the South Face of Half Dome. A storm moved in and drenched the two climbers with waves of cold rain water. They waited, trying to decide what to do. A lull in the storm gave Rowell the break he wanted and he decided to try rappelling.

"I got down one rappel and tested the ropes and couldn't pull them. They were frozen in place. The jumars wouldn't work so it took me about two hours in the middle of the storm, soaked to the skin, to make prusik knots that would freeze each time you stood on them. Then you would pry them apart with your bare fingers and move up. I got back up there, shivering uncontrollably, and here was Harding sitting there pretty comfortably in the BAT tent. He looked pretty smart right then. Our approach to the storm was very different. He just sat down to wait it out and I felt like I had to do something to get out of there."

They were rescued, and years later, Harding was quoted by a reporter as saying that was the closest he had ever come to dying. Rowell said he "asked him if the reporter quoted him right. He said, 'Yes,' but he sure didn't give it away back in 1968. He was very stoic about things."

One can't talk to Galen Rowell very long without the topic turning back to outdoor photography. For him, the combination of climbing and photography is an excellent match. Yet he sees a distinction in the two interests.

"I get some of the same adventure going out and taking photographs, finding new situations, but there is a major difference when you're putting your life on the line. One of the things that really made me go 'aha' were some comments by a biologist who had a theory that the need for human males to put themselves in life-threatening situations and, through their own abilities, to work their way out may be a kind of holdover from the millions of years when our ancestors ventured out in small hunting groups to challenge animals that were much larger than they were. In order to survive, the human race needed these male groups in which people had to risk themselves in times of danger for the good of the clan. If you went up against a mammoth, someone had to go up to it at close range and put a spear into it. The scientist felt there might be some inherited behavior in human beings that was a vestige of those times—'an unfathomable longing' as he described it. I have also read of studies with animals in which an instinct is so weak that it can't be detected in adult animals raised away from reinforcement in the wild at a young age, but when the same animal species is raised in its original habitat, the instinct returns quite strongly. I think the same kind of thing happens with climbers. People who stick with climbing, who don't just climb for three years and then give up, were usually introduced to wilderness at a young age. A lot of top rock climbers will be flashes for a few years then vanish into other activities. People who climb for long periods of time almost always have something in their backgrounds that took them into the mountains when they were young. They have a tie-in with risk and adventure, stemming from a really young age."

For Rowell, the biggest challenge in outdoor photography is "bringing back key images that say what an area or experience really is. Outdoor photography, like climbing, involves thinking out problems and solving them, spending time in the wild and having success or failure. It's much different than just backpacking, where your success is almost guaranteed. Unlike climbing, outdoor photography doesn't usually risk your life. Part of my success has been that I am a participant in the events I record. My camera is there, holding still an instant of time as it happens to me, rather than being a voyeur peeping into somebody else's world."

For climbers wishing to improve their own photography, Rowell offers some words of advice. "If you want to make the break from just bringing back pictures and hoping that some of them are good, to making consistently good photographs, you need to learn to see the world like film sees it, rather than trying to see in human vision and hoping that it is going to translate. Doing that is kind of like learning a foreign language. When you learn how film sees differently than the eye, you'll learn to see light in that different language."

Warren Harding

Born:
June 18, 1924, Oakland, California

Hometown:
Moab, Utah

Occupation:
Retired construction field engineer, writer

Climbing Highlights:
The Nose of El Capitan (first ascent), Wall of the Early Morning
Light (first ascent), East Buttress of Middle Cathedral Rock (first
ascent), Lost Arrow Direct (first ascent), Half Dome (first ascent,
South Face), Mt. Watkins (first ascent, South Face), Keeler
Needle (first ascent), Mt. Conness, and many others

When Warren Harding started up the Nose route on El Capitan, the 3,000-foot face was blank. Not a single climbing route had been done. He had his pick of places to climb and chose a prominent line where two great walls joined, a feature that stands out from many locations in the valley, especially when one face is sunlit and the other in shadow.

In June 1957, Royal Robbins and his team climbed the Northwest Face of Half Dome, a climb Harding had been studying. Harding quickly turned his interest to the other major Yosemite challenge and within weeks, along with Mark Powell and Bill "Dolt" Feuerer, began an ascent they never could have imagined.

Using a system similar to that used in big mountains, they fixed ropes and hauled equipment up the vertical rock. They climbed and rappelled each day, trying to push the route ever higher. By November of that year, they had reached the 1,200-foot level and celebrated Thanksgiving dinner on the Sickle Ledge.

Harding recalled that it was a very slow process. "You must understand that in 1957, rock climbing was still in the cave-man stage. The largest piton was a one-inch angle. A friend of mine made some larger things called bongs. We had four of those to fit the wider cracks."

Harding was thirty-three at this time, with years of construction work behind him. The long hours on the rock and the exposure didn't bother him, but the progress was slow.

"I couldn't say I had great feelings of awe about the route. I did feel, 'There's no way we're going to make this turkey.' We strung out ropes about 1,000 feet so we could come back down. We didn't even realize that that was unethical, and nobody else did either. These climbing ethics were invented later. We were just interested in what we were doing and it went on and on and on. I know that I became obsessed with the project. It never occured to me to just can this thing and go away."

They were unable to finish the climb in 1957 and came back the next summer. Powell injured his ankle and dropped out, as did Feuerer. They were replaced by Rick Calderwood, Wayne Merry, and George Whitmore. Before the end of the summer, Calderwood also dropped out and the remaining team was wearing down. "Finally, toward the end, I was tired," Harding remembered. "That was before jumars, so we were prusiking. In the end, we decided we had to get it done. In twelve continuous days, we polished that turkey off."

On the night of November 11, 1958, Harding climbed through most of the night and reached the rim of El Capitan in the greyness of dawn. The ascent had taken forty-seven days of climbing over eighteen months, and a new age in big wall climbing had been born. However, the epic climbs of Warren Harding were not over yet.

In 1970, he scouted out a route that was one of the most difficult in the area. "I had looked at this route with Glen Denny. We had just failed at an attempt on the South Face of Half Dome, and we were out with a jug of wine, going around the Valley. Our purpose, ostensibly at least, was to find the ultimate climb in the Valley. We settled upon this area of El Capitan, the eastern face. It's just east of the Nose. We argued a little bit and came up with two names. I wanted the Wall of the Early Morning Light and Glen wanted Dawn Wall, so it's known by both names. Nothing more came of that, except I never forgot about it.

"I had been involved in an accident—I was hit by a car at a construction site and it demolished my right leg. That took a while to heal. I was working in the [Yosemite] Valley because I couldn't do my regular construction job. Then I met this fellow, Dean Caldwell. He was more of a mountain climber than a rock climber, but he was good at both. He had badly wrenched an ankle, so it was perfectly safe for us to talk about climbing, because neither one of us could get off the ground." He laughed. "We kept talking and going up to look at this Wall of the Early Morning Light. We both drank a lot and pretty soon we were actually making plans to do this, and by October, we were heading up the wall. We had a lot of storms, and we were not particularly energetic climbers. We didn't try to do things like El Cap in a day.

"There were problems—like we had only planned the food and water for fifteen days. Actually water was never a problem because we had a lot coming down." He laughed. "Food became a problem. Day fifteen found us somewhat less than halfway up. We were in constant communication with the ground people. We even had a ground manager and we assured them that we were okay. For one thing, we couldn't quite figure out how we would get down, since it was constantly overhanging wall. We kept going and going and going. Day twenty we were up quite a ways further and the climbing looked like it got a little faster going. We even had a party on the Wine Tower. Dean pointed out that we were on the only ledge in 2,700 feet, so we broke out a bottle of Christian Brothers Cabernet Sauvignon and we had some scraps of cheese. We were semi-subsidized by Christian Brothers Winery." He laughed. "We even had a crystal wine glass.

"There had been an increasing amount of aerial activity, and we wondered what that was all about. We heard sounds from above and people down below yelling up, and we determined that we were being rescued. We got busy and sent down nasty notes that we wouldn't have anything to do with a rescue, so call it off. Finally, we did get the assurance that there would be no rescue attempt, which would have been ridiculous. We were in fine shape, not much food, but we were going fine. From then on, the media just wouldn't leave this thing alone. When we topped out seven days later [twenty-seven total days], there must have been about one hundred media people on top. After we got through with them and they had their film in a can, we went to the valley and had a party. We had phone calls from all over, including New York. 'Would you come to New York and be on *Wide World of Sports*?' Why not? We spent two days in New York City talking with Howard Cosell."

Most of Harding's climbing has focused on El Capitan, but he has enjoyed others. He explained, "My favorite route in the Valley is the Direct on the Lost Arrow. I want to go back and do that again. It's the only route I've ever wanted to repeat. I don't think there is a bad climb. In all honesty, I can say I have enjoyed every climb I have done, in retrospect—the more retro, the spect." He laughed.

Although his climbs have been serious commitments, he does not seem to take climbing, or perhaps anything else, too seriously. "I was on a lecture tour back east when I got a message that Prentice-Hall wanted to see me," he recalled. "I thought, 'What! Write a book? Well, sure, but the trouble is, I don't know how.'" The editor wanted to find a ghostwriter, but Harding replied, "I have a certain style and nobody else can write for me."

Harding did write the book titled *Downward Bound*, which he characterized as "an unlikely title for a climbing treatise. I take a rather tongue-in-cheek attitude towards climbing.

"I get interviewed a lot by television and magazine people. I love the intense way they come on. Their eyes are glistening and they say, 'Harding, what does it take to do this thing?' I say, 'I think stupidity plays a big part of it.' And I'm not really being that facetious. I think you have to be stupid to spend that much time beating yourself, when you could very well get killed or something. However, I wouldn't change any of this for the world.

"I've been doing some heavy duty stuff for more than thirty years, and I've come close to buying the farm a couple of times that I know of. Now how many times I got by without realizing what was happening—who knows? It can be extremely dangerous if you don't know what you are doing. If you're competent, then it's still dangerous, but not *that* dangerous. I would say that statistically, rock climbing is very safe. This doesn't hold true for Himalayan climbing. That's an entirely different ball game. On the other hand, people get injured all the time playing football. The nice thing about climbing is that you can do it all your life, whereas very few people can play football past thirty or thirty-five."

On the occasions where Harding found himself in dangerous situations and possibly facing death, he said he wasn't afraid. He recalled a time when he was on the South Face of Half Dome in 1968. "Galen [Rowell] and I had been pinned down for three days and my weather-proof BAT tents were anything but weather proof. We were soaking wet at about 9,000 feet elevation. Ice was falling outside these tents and inside it was a degree or two warmer." He laughed. "You can only do induced shivering for so long and then you collapse from exhaustion.

"It seemed that with the deteriorating weather and the resulting drop in temperature, we wouldn't make it through the night. I felt prepared that this was it. I felt really peaceful. Now this could be construed as some great psychological experiment or something, but I was probably so tired I didn't give a shit. Now I've read that people close to death get this peaceful, serene feeling. I think I was just tired and didn't care. I am not a religious man. I had no religious upbringing, so I had nothing to fear—no devils to attack me. I would simply be gone. But our Mayday radio calls were answered that night and we were jumaring up out of there with a rescue headed up by Royal Robbins. Had they not got there, I think it could have turned out rather differently, because I just didn't care anymore. I guess you get that way after a while."

It took five trips back to the South Face of Half Dome before Harding finally finished the climb. That effort and the climbs on the Nose and Wall of the Early Morning Light on El Capitan demonstrate the Harding style. He has been able to push beyond the accepted limits of human endurance in establishing new routes.

"I must have some inner drive that keeps me going," he surmised. "On some climbs, hey, I could have turned back, but I kept going. Sometimes I got in a heap of trouble, but somehow I came out of it. Perhaps the greatest exemplification would be how I kept the Nose thing going for a year and a half, spending a lot of money and a lot of energy. I don't seem like a terribly driven person, but I guess somewhere in there there's a little drive. That's what it is—it's drive that puts up climbs. For example, [Royal] Robbins is, was, always will be a hard-driving man.

"Where climbing is going in the future, I couldn't possibly conjecture, because I'm still trying to grasp what is happening now, and not so much the mechanical things, but the advances in free climbing. When I started out, I was fairly good. I wasn't any athlete. I was just one step above your skid-row wino. Now we have people that are of Olympic caliber. I don't even know who the top people are right now, they come and go so quickly, but I think what they are doing is fantastic. I look at it in total awe.

"I admire it all, even the mechanical. Now I'm the last person on earth who should be critical of mechanical aids. For a while I thought I was drawing the line by saying I wouldn't use Friends, these crack jumars, and then I opened another jug of wine and did a little self-examination and said, 'Hey, you're getting just like the people who used to criticize you.' And I had another slug of wine and said, 'The hell with it. I will draw the line at *buying* Friends, because I have friends who have Friends. At fifty dollars a copy, I'm not going to buy that shit. That was as close to an ethical crisis as I've ever come." He laughed.

In the early eighties, Harding was invited to England by the British Mountaineering Council to give a series of lectures. At one of the meetings he met Henry Barber, who had done many significant climbs himself. Of Barber, Harding said, "From his writings, I was convinced I wouldn't like the guy at all, but we seemed to hit it off quite well. He was familiar with my situation as an aging, controversial climber and he suggested that I simply start over. And I said, 'You know, Henry, that's a terrific idea.' And at over sixty years of age, I'm off to Yosemite for some moving up and down the trails. I was going to say running, but maybe I won't run."

Patrik Callis

Born:
March 17, 1938, Ontario, Oregon
Hometown:
Bozeman, Montana
Occupation:
Chemistry professor
Climbing Highlights:
Jiazi (China, first ascent, South Ridge), Mt. Index (first winter
ascent of North Peak), Mt. Robson (first ascent of North Face),
Lost Arrow Direct (Yosemite, first ascent), Great White Throne
(first ascent, Southwest Face), Green Gully (frozen waterfall, first
ascent). Twenty-five of the initial forty first ascents on Suicide
Rock and many ice and rock climbs near Bozeman. Wrote first
climber's guidebook to Suicide Rock

"I can trace the desire to climb back to a very young age, maybe six or seven,"
Pat Callis said. "I know I felt that urge then. I remember saying to my dad when
we were swimming in the ocean, which was something I didn't particularly enjoy,
'Let's go climb that mountain.' "

Yet Callis's desire to climb went unfulfilled for several years. He heard stories
about the dangers of climbing and believed them. Still, an occasional mountain
photo in a magazine would stir an emotion and his curiosity would be aroused
once again.

"When I was a sophomore in high school, the English teacher was a climber.
He showed us a section in a literature book on climbing Everest that gave a sketch
of the English attempts to climb it. It was still unclimbed at that time, of course,
and that was very romantic. It really gripped me.

"As part of that, he showed some slides of climbing trips on nearby vol-
canoes—on the North Sister, I think. Oregon is noted for these beautiful volca-
noes—they really stand out. They are very attractive and very alluring. I assumed
that those things were straight up and down, but when he showed these slides I
realized that it wasn't anything like that at all. It was like hiking above timberline.
I was surprised at how reasonable it was, that climbing didn't have to be a daredevil
sort of thing. From that point on, I read book after book and my dad was nice
enough to schedule us to do a tenderfoot climb. We did the Middle Sister. It was
something that occupied my emotional being from then on. I can't explain exactly
why, it was just something I wanted to do all the time.

"I was never good at other sports. This was the one thing I was really good at. I felt naturally at home in the mountains. It turned me on and I was good, not only from a technical point of view, but I had a sense of where to go."

Callis, who appears in a two-page picture on Green Gully in Chouinard's book, *Climbing Ice*, has enjoyed a wide range of climbing experiences. "That's partly because I got started going up snow peaks and learned the ice axe and crampon bit even before I learned rock climbing," he explained. "The first rock climbing I ever did was on Jefferson, which has a little rock climbing at the very top after several thousand feet of snow. It was my second climb."

After more rock climbing and mountaineering, Callis discovered ice climbing and knew it was something he would enjoy. "I got really excited about ice climbing about the same time everybody else did. Around 1970, when Chouinard put out ice tools that were more adaptive, I really identified with that. I'd long wanted to do the same thing. Front-pointing was a wonderful, natural thing for me. Even with the hinged crampons that were available in the sixties, I loved to go front-pointing up things, and the heck with steps—much to the dismay of some of the older climbers who were with me. I always thought that it was a shame that ice axes weren't curved, and yet I would never think of changing the traditional axe. I had played around a little with a hammer that had a hook on it. I could see the need for that very clearly, but I didn't take any action on it, so when he [Chouinard] did it, I just jumped on it and said, 'This is wonderful. I know just what to do with this.' And I immediately went out and started climbing fairly steep waterfalls.

"At that time, none of these waterfalls had been discovered by climbers, so we had a really nice period of time where we were finding these things and climbing them, and they were all first ascents. The waterfalls here weren't as long and steep as some of the things in Canada, and I sometimes wished I had gone up there. We were in a position to go up there, and we could have copped a lot of first ascents then. That was largely because of the job I have. I don't have that much free time, so the climbs that I have done were always carefully selected, and a lot of times were with people who were very professional climbers who were well positioned to know what thing to do, like Fred Beckey and Warren Harding. I've been very fortunate that of the climbs that I have done, the percentage of good climbs is very high, because I didn't live to climb all summer like many people. It's kind of a compromise I have made."

After high school, Callis, like many climbers, had some tough decisions to make. "I knew I wanted to go to college and learn a lot of things, but I wasn't sure. I knew I loved the outdoors and was thinking in terms of game management or forestry, but intellectually those things were not what I was after. I had always gravitated towards chemistry. So I've always had two passions. Finally, I justified it at one point in that I said it does make sense in a way to have a contrast. If you're going to be in a lab working all the time, when you get out, it will be really wonderful. But if you are already out there, it will be a busman's holiday. I've seen guides get pretty burned out on it. I've enjoyed that contrast."

It wasn't always easy for Callis to keep up his climbing and still meet the demands of university teaching and research.

"When I was at the point of making these sorts of career-oriented decisions, it wasn't very customary for people to just go out and climb, be a climbing bum, so to speak, whereas in the seventies, lots of people started doing that with the affluence that came over the country.

"When I was nearing the end of graduate school, I was feeling unhappy, because I felt climbing was such an important part of my life. At the same time, I couldn't give up the pursuit of this physical chemistry, the physical insights into nature that that gives. I found that gripping, also. It's always been a little bit of an uncomfortable thing. It's like serving two masters. On either side of the fence, you're not doing what you could do. You can always see potential that is not being fulfilled the way it would be if you were putting everything into it.

"I went on sabbatical to Cornell University and I was in a frame of mind at that time to give up climbing, to view it as a much less important part of my life. Instead, I would really dive into chemistry. But it didn't really work out. I didn't really feel very happy. After a few months, I started going ice climbing there and met some climbers and I was terribly out of shape. Mentally, I could hardly lead. My arms would get tired. In the spring, we went to the Shawangunks. Since then I've brought myself back to the level that I was before. I was always able to climb at about the standard level in the country. Now of course, I'm back up there, but the standard level is about three grades higher.

"I felt a surge of strength coming back both in climbing and in chemistry after coming back from the sabbatical. It was pretty stimulating, particularly afterward, trying to absorb all the new material. I recognized that it was happening and I didn't try to exclude one or the other."

One particular climb had a big impact on Callis. His first ascent (with Dan Davis) of the north face of Mt. Robson in the Canadian Rockies "was such a sought-after plum. We had read articles in the *Alpine Journal* and accounts by Beckey and Chouinard and other climbers, one of which said the north face of Robson might as well be the Eiger or something. Here was this thing that was really hyped up in our minds to be an ultimate climb. Davis called me up and said, 'Do you want to go to Robson?' To me, doing Robson by any route would be a big thing. At the same time, in the back of my mind, I was thinking the north face and Dan was, too. We knew Beckey had been trying it, so I called him and said, 'We want to go to Robson and we'd like to climb with you on it.' Beckey, though, plans his summers very tightly and I had a tight schedule, too, so it worked out that we couldn't be there at the same time. We went into Robson with the advice from everyone we had talked to along the way. It had been snowing all summer and the mountain was in horrible shape. People said we'd never get up there and had better wait. It was true for all sides of the mountain except for the north face. It was the one side that was frozen. It had this snow on it which made it easier to climb, perhaps, than it would have been normally. It was late enough in the summer that it was cold and there weren't many rockfall dangers. We got up it and it was such a funny feeling. We did it. That was early in my career, and it had a very big effect on me."

The expedition to Jiazi in China made Callis think about his climbing in different ways. "It was a very nice peak and it wasn't easy to find the best way up. It was interesting exploration just to find the proper route. I did have some apprehension because of my family. There was a sacrifice in terms of income, and it tore me up because in some ways, it seemed selfish to do that kind of thing and I don't like to think of myself as selfish. Yet, I thought, if I don't do this, I just won't be happy with myself. It was expensive in all kinds of ways.

"I've often thought that a person who doesn't know much about climbing must think it is just crazy, somewhat like race car driving at a professional level. I don't believe that it has to be like that. It is for people who go out without the proper instruction or just go out cold and get themselves into trouble. I believe that the dangers are somewhat similar to driving cars on highways. The potential for destruction is about the same in terms of head-on collisions or falling off something. The business of driving is treated with a lot of training and regulation and equipment development. You don't even have to come close to that kind of preparation for climbing to be just as safe as driving.

"The question of why a person climbs does come up as if it were a legitimate question, but I don't think it's really any more legitimate than why somebody plays tennis. I know that the reason that people ask it is because it is considered dangerous. That is the popular perception. You know—why you would risk your life—and my answer to that is you are risking your life when you go on the highway. Climbing is something that has a great deal of excitement to it and many facets of pleasure, going all the way from flowers and streams and weather and beauty that is associated with most of these places, to the movement of the body that the gymnast and runner find so enjoyable. This is an integration of all that, plus the survival thing. You can say, 'Well, I just don't care,' which is a very European attitude—they drive that way, too. Americans tend to be more safety-oriented. My climbing has fallen into that mold. I never did much solo climbing. I was always very well protected and when you do it that way, it's no more dangerous than driving. You can drive dangerously and pass on curves or you can drive in a way that is less risky. You have that same choice in climbing and that in itself is satisfying in its own way.

"It's extremely complex. It's the same reason that people in all kinds of areas do things that are creative in a sense. This includes gymnastics, for example, inventing new tricks, being the first one to do a new move, or creating art, writing novels. It's something that gets into your blood, this business of climbing a piece of rock or ice that has never been done before. There is quite a close parallel to it in scientific research. You get the same thrill discovering new knowledge, new facts, new ways to do things. That's one part of it, but not all people who climb get into that. Some are quite content to climb what has already been climbed.

"I got introduced to this thing of new routes, the creative aspect and that became pretty gripping. It's just there and you don't know why. It is a pure emotional attraction. I've thought about it over the years as to why it's there and I've told some people that our genes are not really very different than they were a mere three or four thousand years ago. I don't think physically we have evolved as fast as our lifestyle has changed. I think there is something really bad about our lifestyles generally these days in that we are very soft. You don't have to work that hard to exist, whereas it wasn't that long ago when people moved out of the eastern seaboard into the west and had to face severe challenges just to live. What you did then really meant something. If you didn't get the crops planted or have successful hunts you were in trouble. Since that has always been the case until recently, I think we are still genetically selective for that type of existence. I think that a lot of unhappiness or anxieties that people experience in today's way of life stem from this transplanted being that is really not programmed to cope with things.

"There's something really satisfying about climbing. You are able to play this game in which you step into a course of action in which, once you commit yourself to it, the rules are pretty much like surviving. It's kind of a miniature game of life in the prehistoric times where the things that you do matter. It's not all that dangerous. You usually know you can go back when the situations get bad and are pretty intense. When it's over, it's wonderfully satisfying."

Still climbing hard routes at over fifty years of age, Callis likes to joke about the aging athlete. "As a visitor from England once put it, the kinds of things you can do now are coming into the category of 'remarkable for your age'." He laughed. "It's hard to adapt to that, but I'm starting to play that game more and more. Maybe 5.12 isn't out of reach. Maybe Everest—I know Everest isn't out of reach. I just don't know whether I can ever get myself on an Everest expedition. I know I've got the ability to do good things on Everest, but I don't know if I can stand the wrenching of leaving the family for the time it would take to climb Everest. I have that hope, but I'm not actively going after it."

Callis also has a sense that he was in the right place at the right time in his development as a climber.

"I feel sorry for the young climbers in a way, because relative to what I was able to experience—well, there was a lot of unplowed ground and it was exciting to be into that—and now it would appear on the surface that that doesn't exist. Also, there are so many people climbing that you are just one among thousands and thousands, and you don't get the heady recognition that you could get then. A climber of my ability and intensity starting out now would not make any impact at all. The availability of significant things to do is greatly diminished, and that's not unique to climbing. It's happened to virtually every human activity there is. It drives a lot of people out prematurely who were around during a golden age and had a lot of fun doing things and getting a lot of recognition for it. It can be distasteful to those who knew how it used to be.

"Still, what gets done is dictated by what has been done. The levels of achievement just keep going on in orders of magnitude beyond what anybody's imagination can deal with and it happens so gradually. It seems that those who are faced with what has been done automatically rise to that level, more or less without great struggle and do things that represented a psychological limit to those that came before. The mind is an important factor in this. You get ideas about what can and cannot be done. That's what really stops things from happening. I expect that there are a lot more adventures out there waiting for young climbers than I can imagine."

Finis Mitchell

Born:
November 14, 1901, Ethel, Missouri

Hometown:
Rock Springs, Wyoming

Occupation:
Retired railroader, state legislator

Climbing Highlights:
277 peaks in the Wind River Mountains of Wyoming, including Mitchell, Square Top, Gannett, War Bonnet, Mt. Ladd, Mt. Bonneville, Big Sandy, Dog Tooth, and others. Wrote guide book to Wind River Mountains

When the mapmakers from the United States Geological Survey were finishing the maps for the Wind River Mountains, they called Finis Mitchell. And for good reason. He knows those mountains better than any other human being and, in fact, named a majority of the features himself.

Mitchell estimates that in his explorations he has hiked 15,000 miles, named a "list of lakes a mile long," taken 126,000 slides (each carefully numbered and indexed), worn out twelve 35mm cameras, and climbed 277 peaks since he started in 1909.

His first climb was on an elk hunt with his father. "He wasn't a climber," explained Mitchell. "He was just a worker trying to make a living for a family. I was the oldest boy and I was always with him. We had walked around a lot, and I got to where I wanted to see what was on the mountain."

Mitchell had to quit school in seventh grade because his father became sick. He never returned, but his adventures in the Wind River Mountains have meant more to him than any schooling could have meant. "I wouldn't trade my experience in those mountains for the biggest lawyer's fees in the world," he said. "I'm all right the way I am."

In the Depression, Mitchell, with his father and brothers, ran a fishing camp and decided to stock several lakes with fish. They used six horses and twelve five-gallon milk cans to haul fish up into the mountains.

"When we stocked those lakes, they were virgin waters. They were lousy with food. When we first turned those fish loose, we didn't know any better. Some of them just gorged themselves. Some of the German browns got up to ten and twelve pounds because there was so much food. The brook trout in Middle Fork Lake got up to six and a quarter pounds. The rainbows got up to four, five, and six pounds."

Altogether, they stocked 314 lakes with two and a half million trout over an eight year period. The fish from these lakes, in turn, populated some 700 lakes in all.

"The reason I wrote the book [*Wind River Trails*] was to tell people how to get in and find all these fish. I wanted the people to know what was theirs, and it really is theirs. All these lakes and mountains belong to the people and they should get out and use them and preserve them for future generations. I've put on hundreds of shows for the schools and those kids get interested. They listen and they remember. They often ask, 'Who owns all that land, Mr. Mitchell?' and I say, 'Why, you do. You own it. It is public land and you should take care of it.' "

Mitchell loves to share his love of the land with people everywhere. He has given lectures in New York, San Francisco, Portland, Seattle, Denver, Chicago, and elsewhere. In 1976 alone, he gave forty-four lectures and asked only for expense money in return. He signs his letters "With Kindness to Mankind," and this love of the mountains and people led him to a different kind of adventure.

"The editor of the *Rock Springs Rocket* came to me and said, 'The way you think about people, Mitch, why don't you run for the legislature and have something to do with making the laws.' I decided it would be an honor to go, but instead of campaigning, I went down to take pictures of that Echo Park Area where they're digging up all the fossils. I didn't campaign at all, but in the election I got three times as many votes as I ever thought I would.

"The first thing that happened when I got to Cheyenne was that they presented me with a set of Wyoming statutes [law books]. That was more education than I ever dreamed of having. I ran for a second term and thought it was nice. I got paid good money and had a leave of absence, but I found out that certain cliques control everything. The committees have chairmen, and every bill that you present goes to that committee. If you introduce a bill—it doesn't matter how much it might benefit the American people—if their clique doesn't like it, they cubby-hole it. I decided I wouldn't run for a third term. I was wasting my time. I thought I could use my time to better advantage in the wilderness areas.

"I've always been one to admire creation. God created us all equal. We're all human beings. I think that the Good Lord intended for everyone to live equally. It hasn't worked out that way, but I don't want to start talking politics."

Mitchell has been likened to a one-man Chamber of Commerce for the Wind River Mountains and his efforts have not gone unnoticed. He has received the Joseph W. Penfield award from the Izaak Walton League for his long commitment to conservation, the Outstanding Achievement Award from the United States Environmental Protection Agency, the United States Department of Agriculture Forest Service Award, and enough other certificates and letters from congressmen and officials to fill several scrapbooks. Pinedale, a town at the base of his beloved mountains, honored him with a Finis Mitchell Day, and the University of Wyoming recently gave him an honorary doctorate. Of these honors, Mitchell said, "Man can do wonders with God as his helper."

For most of his life, Mitchell has climbed alone. "I would try to get someone to go with me and all I could ever get out of them was, 'I haven't lost anything up there.' Once in a while, someone would go with me, and I guess it was my fault. I was so healthy and so strong that I could just run in those mountains. Sometimes someone would go with me and they would never go again. I wondered why. It was because I walked the tail off them. Even today, with me well over eighty years old, I hear people say, 'Don't ever go climbing with that old S.O.B.. He'll walk you to death.' That's wrong because I have to take it easy. Now I hold people up. Serves me right for walking people to death before. By myself I don't have to worry about anybody. When I get tired, I sit down on a rock.

"I'm getting along all right. I'm pretty finicky about what I eat. I'm particular about my health. I never touch pepper or salt or spices. I just don't like them. I'm going to try to live a few more years so I'll have a good excuse to kiss all the good-looking gals that congratulate me on my hundredth birthday." He laughed. "I believe you don't stop hiking because you grow old. You grow old because you stop hiking."

Mitchell told of a time in 1952 when he went on a seventeen-day solo hike. "I started out with seventy-eight pounds and got into trouble at what I named Suicide Lake. I fell down and broke my tripod, ruined my food and didn't think I could get back out. The mountain had slid and the rocks were bigger than houses. I had to crawl like a rock chuck. I made up my mind that if I ever got out of there alive, and I didn't think I would, I was going to name that lake Suicide Lake, and the government maps have that name on them today."

On another trip in 1960, he ran into a blizzard. "The whole country was nothing but a mass of snow. I took a picture of some sheep—the rams are leaning over against the wind. I followed the sheep down onto the ledges, and there were fifty or sixty sheep down in there already—ewes, lambs, and everything. I went right on in with them. Sometimes they walked up within six feet of my sleeping bag."

Searching for difficult routes was never of interest to Mitchell. With his camera and an assortment of lenses, he looked at summits as vantage points for more photographs that eventually became a series of post cards he often gives away when he meets people.

"I've hardly ever used a rope. You don't use ropes when you're alone, and almost all of my climbing has been alone. You can get up them without ropes if you do it carefully. I just like to climb. If I'm alone, that's all right. If I'm with someone, they have to put up with a lot of jabbering.

"I don't object to them drilling holes and tearing up the face of the mountains like they do in Yosemite, but they don't have to do that. I've climbed 277 peaks since 1909 and I've always found some way up them.

"I just took an old quilt to sleep with and a tarp. I didn't know what plastic was. I didn't know what down sleeping bags were until I got some Army surplus ones. I've slept sitting in a hole with my feet on one rock and my head on another on the glaciers. Now the equipment has changed so much. It makes it kind of sissyfied."

His knowledge of the Wind River Mountains is encyclopaedic. Every question about a lake, stream or mountain brings an instant response. "I don't think there is a square mile up there where I haven't been," he asserted. "I've been at this a long time, a lot of years. I've named a lot of places. In fact, in the Downs Mountain quadrangle, I named everything. I explored the whole area. It's away from Gannett and the early explorers climbed the bigger peaks."

Mitchell has lived to see a mountain named after him, a rare tribute. "A guy from the Forest Service talked to me about this. He found out that they have a ruling that no land feature should be named for a human being unless that person had done something unusual or outstanding for the people. We had stocked all those fish—that was for the people. He asked what was my favorite spot in the Wind Rivers and I told him that I thought from that peak [Mt. Mitchell] you had the best view of the Cirque of the Towers. It's right at the end, and when you are up there, you can see the whole cirque.

"I love the mountains. They are man's sole salvation, if he could but see when he looks. If we would rid ourselves of greed and selfishness, why, the world would take care of itself. I'm proud of the life I've lived."

Alison Osius

Born:

July 26, 1958, Oakland, California

Hometown:

Aspen, Colorado

Occupation:

Editor for *Climbing* magazine, lecturer

Climbing Highlights:

Numerous rock climbs up to 5.12 in the eastern and western United States, in Scotland, Wales, France, Australia, Italy, and Canada. Guide in Wales, California, Washington, and New Hampshire. Member of the Board of directors of the American Alpine Club. Climbing competitions in Italy, Great Britain, Arizona, and Utah

As a climbing guide in North Wales, Alison Osius had the chance to see a film called *Break on Through*, which featured an ascent of The Naked Edge, a 5.11 rock climb in El Dorado Canyon, Colorado.

She watched the lead climber wildly struggling to get up the final crack, slip, and launch into mid-air. She watched as the film repeated the fall several times. She was intrigued by the movie and by the route.

"I remember looking at that climb and realizing that I would never be able to climb it," she recalled. "There are some things in this world that you will never be able to do, and I didn't dare think I could ever do that climb."

She climbed every day that summer and pushed her level up to 5.10. Still, she wouldn't let herself think that she could possibly climb The Naked Edge.

She worked as a guide the next summer, and the next, and finally, while driving through Colorado, she got a chance to see the famous route. Rain prevented much climbing that trip. Of her thoughts at that time, she explained, "I did realize that it was something I could probably do, but I still wanted to wait. If something is really classic, you don't want to be up there falling off and thrashing around. You want to go up and have a good day on it."

Two years later she climbed The Naked Edge. "I had actually waited too long, because I didn't have much doubt about getting up it. It was an anticlimax."

She paused, thinking of the climb. "It's hard when you attain your dreams sometimes—they lose some of their grandeur. But that's the way it is. You just have to find new dreams. Still, no climb has meant as much to me as The Naked Edge."

Osius, who has a master's degree from Columbia University School of Journalism, didn't set out to be a climber. She was studying at Middlebury College in Vermont and working on the school newspaper when, at her first editorial board meeting, the editor suggested a story on climbing.

"I just blurted out, 'I'll do that,' " she remembered. "He gave me a list of people to interview, so I went around to their houses and dorm rooms and talked to them. I really liked their 'war stories,' and I really liked them. They were characters, so modest and unaffected. They weren't very impressed with themselves and they were very funny. They were also very gracious to me, although I was asking some dumb questions. Anyway, those people ended up being role models for me and I started climbing with them. Over the years they became my best friends at school."

In her senior year at college, Osius found herself too busy to take full days to go climbing, but she wanted to get some exercise, so she helped organize a women's rugby club.

"I had to give my thesis defense with a black eye, and I broke my nose, but rugby was a great chance to go out and be animalistic for awhile," she recalled. "I played in the second row of the scrum and was scrum leader. I loved being on a team. I hadn't been on a team since high school. It was fun because I was always with these people and we had something to talk about. It made me think more about climbing as a team effort."

Osius did try ice climbing, although she spent most of her climbing time on vertical rock. From ice climbing, she learned that "I can't take the cold at all. I climb badly in cold weather. I have a thing called Reynaud's Disease. My capillaries shut down when I get cold, like below sixty degrees. It's not a serious thing, just that my fingers and toes go numb and hurt and turn white. When I got frostbite on some of my toes, the doctor said to never go again. I was always afraid of frostbiting my fingers and wrecking my rock climbing."

Just how important rock climbing is to her became clear when she developed tendonitis in her elbows. "I went climbing anyway," she said. "I realized that I was out there for different reasons than in the past. I wasn't pushing. I wasn't trying to improve and do ever harder climbs. I was strictly out there to be with my friends and have fun and it was great. The people that you climb with are more important than the route you do, anyway. I was thinking, what if my elbows get worse? Is there anything else I could switch into? I couldn't think of anything I wanted to do as much as climb.

"I used to be a competitive windsurfer, but I got bored with that because you're out there by yourself. There's a lot of standing still, holding the same tack. Also, there's no dialogue. Maybe you can shout at another windsurfer, but not a lot."

Osius has written for *Outside, Ultrasport, Skiing, Climbing, Rock and Ice, Backpacker, Mountain*, the *Washington Post Magazine*, and many other publications. "The thing I like about climbing is that there is dialogue," she explained. "How many people talk to each other when they're in a ski race? When you're climbing, it is often dramatic or funny and you're talking to each other. That's why I continue to write about climbing.

"I used to ski a lot and work as a ski instructor. I really love it, but it's the same motion. Granted, some people do that same motion very well, but it's turn, turn, turn. Climbing is never the same. All climbs are different so I never get bored with it. Every climb is a different puzzle to figure out and takes a different combination, a different series, of moves. The part I like the best is the figuring out. You figure out what you'll do—my right hand there, my left hand there, my right foot there—and then you have to perform what you figured, and sometimes you even have to perform it fast or you'll fall off."

Osius has entered several climbing competitions. She said, "I've never had any problem with the idea of competition at all. Some people say, *'Competition—you're involved in competition?'* and they pretend to shoot a gun at me. I grew up racing sailboats with my family and admiring the ski runs of Jean Claude Killy and never thought of it as anything but good.

"I don't think competition will make any difference in climbing, or at least it will be minimal, because the competitions will never involve anything but a small percentage of climbers. Those people can go and compete. Who are they hurting, especially when it's done on artificial walls? They're not chipping holds in rock. They're not bringing huge crowds out to a natural environment to stomp on plants and things.

"The competition might help women's climbing. In fact, women's climbing is really coming into its own, with more and more women climbing all the time. I'd still like to see more out there. Right now there aren't many women climbing really hard climbs, but the more that get out there, the harder they will climb and the more Lynn Hills there will be."

Osius is not just interested in the developments of the sport today. "The history of climbing is important to me. It has a very rich literary tradition, and I'm interested in what Joe Brown did and what Henry Barber did, because we have to remember to judge people in the context of the time in which they were climbing and keep it in perspective. I read a lot of the books and articles, from Maurice Herzog to Henry's [Barber] biography. A lot of the guys who climbed in the last decade or so often don't like the tactics of today's climbers, the hang-dogging and other things. I think the young guys respect what the climbers did in the past and I think that the guys who climbed then ought to respect what is going on now. I wouldn't say the tricksters or the traditionalists are better. It's just different."

One incident in particular helped Osius put climbing in perspective for herself. "I remember when a friend of mine got killed climbing. His father and my father had been classmates in the same college and Mr. Johnson wrote my dad—my dad must have written him a sympathy letter—a lovely letter. He said, 'One thing I hope is that you won't discourage Alison from climbing or try to stop her, because I saw a lot of very good and important things develop in my son through climbing and I saw those same traits in his climbing friends.'

"A lot of it is not just what happens on the rock. Much of it is being part of a team and encouraging each other. Sometimes I have this feeling of being incredibly lucky. A lot of people don't get to do this, don't get the opportunity to learn how. You look around and it's so pretty. The hills, the trees, and mountains are all around you. You find something that is larger than your life and you can take from that and put it into your life. There is such a bonding with people—trusting, sharing, and communicating. It's a nice balance to your daily life. It makes your life much richer."

Lynn Hill
Born:
January 3, 1961, Detroit, Michigan
Hometown:
New Paltz, New York
Occupation:
Professional free climber
and technical advisor
Climbing Highlights:
1984 American Alpine Club Award for Outstanding
Achievement in Mountaineering/Rock Climbing. First place in all
four "Survival of the Fittest" competitions held for women.
Winner of nine out of twelve international climbing competitions
held since 1986, including first place at the Gran Prix de France
D'Escalade, Troubat, France, 1986 and 1987; first place at the
World Championships at Arco, Italy, 1987 and 1988; first place
at the World Indoor Championships at Grenoble, France, 1987;
first place at the International Climbing Championships at
Marseille, 1988; first place at the Masters Competition in Paris,
1988 and 1989; and first place in the German Free Climbing
Championships, 1989

Some climbers like to dabble—a little rock climbing, a mountaineering expedition or two, bouldering, and sometimes a bit of vertical ice. Not Lynn Hill.

"At this time in my life, I'm very focused on free climbing," she affirmed. "I may do some mountaineering later on, but right now it's too difficult to go to the mountains and stay fit for free climbing. I really enjoy movement on rock. Hard free climbs are like a combination of gymnastic moves and a form of dance. I also like the problem-solving aspect of figuring out the sequence of moves. The most difficult routes require a lot of strength and total focus, mentally, physically, and emotionally."

Hill grew up in California and started climbing at Joshua Tree with her older brother and sister when she was fourteen. She tried climbing at other areas and realized that variety would be important in developing her climbing skills.

"Climbing in different parts of the world is not only more interesting, but it has increased my ability to adapt to different types of rock such as limestone, granite, and sandstone. Certainly this is an important asset for on-sight climbing."

Considered by many to be the best woman rock climber in the world, Hill has thought seriously about how climbers develop their skills. "It's hard to put your finger on what quality makes a person climb two grades harder than the average, but in my case, it was probably a lucky combination of genetics, personality, and environment.

"I came from a very athletic family, and my parents were supportive of my involvement in such activities. It also has to do with my approach to climbing. I have a certain sense of body awareness that allows me to position my body correctly on the rock. I also happen to be a visual thinker, good with three-dimensional space, which enables me to plan moves in advance. But the most important factor is desire. I love to climb."

As a young girl, Hill was considered a "tomboy." "I climbed a lot of trees and did things most girls didn't do. I knew I was different, but I enjoyed doing these things. Fortunately, my lack of conformity has allowed me to develop into a well-balanced athlete. Most women have less upper body strength so they tend to use balance and finesse more. Most women are more flexible than most men, so they will approach a climb much differently than men will. Men tend to muscle their way up in a tight situation whereas women tend to be more patient and figure out a more energy-efficient way of going about it. I think this reflects our cultural pressures—men are more likely to be macho about leading and pushing themselves, and women are more inclined to follow a boyfriend and not take risks. This is a very general statement, because this type of risk-taking behavior is not instilled in little girls. I think things are starting to change. Women are realizing that sports are a good way of changing those qualities in themselves. Climbing requires a high strength to weight ratio, not a high degree of absolute power. A football player needs to have a lot of raw power and it doesn't matter what his strength to weight ratio is, but in climbing, it does make a significant difference."

Since the first international climbing competition was held in 1985, Americans have participated, but none have been as successful as Lynn Hill. "Competitions are a new form of climbing that tends to bring out the best or the worst in a climber. The cameras, lights, shouts from the audience and the inevitable shots of adrenaline one experiences in competition can be very distracting. I try to stay relaxed and use this stimulus in a positive way in order to perform my best.

"Competition offers something that I think many climbers want, and certainly the money is helpful. I think artificial climbing walls are the wave of the future because it's possible to have a competition that is fairly well-controlled. Weather is not a problem. You can avoid cheating because you can isolate people so that they can't see others climb. A route can be designed to be as difficult as necessary without chipping holds on a natural rock. On artificial walls, it is possible to design whatever kind of climb you like. The only drawback currently is that it lacks the various features that you find on natural rock. In the future, wall designers could create panels with more divots, dimples, and more three-dimensional forms in order to make it more like natural rock."

Talk of competition naturally leads to the Olympics and Hill thinks rock climbing in the Games is a good possibility. "I don't know how soon, but there is talk of having a demonstration event in the 1992 Winter Games in France. I'm sure there are a lot of people who would love to see this happen, including myself. However, much preparation work needs to be done."

Hill lives with her husband, Russ Raffa, and her dog, Apollo, in the Shawangunk Mountains of New York. To complete climbs of Olympic caliber, she is regularly climbing, running, bouldering, and working out on a climbing simulator. In addition to her work as a technical consultant, she is writing a book on the art of free climbing and giving slide shows and lectures across the country.

Todd Skinner

Born:
October 28, 1958, Sun Valley, Idaho

Hometown:
Pinedale, Wyoming

Occupation:
Professional rock climber

Climbing Highlights:
Russian Speed Climbing Championships (three bronze medals in individual long event, dual event, and overall team standings), El Capitan, Salathe Wall (first free ascent), Calling All the Heroes (first ascent, 5.13d), Gunfighter (first ascent, 5.13 +), and many other first ascents of 5.12 and 5.13 difficulty. Hard rock climbs in Poland, Czechoslovakia, Russia, East Germany, Ireland, Greece, Egypt, Norway, England, Germany, France, Italy, and most rock areas in the United States

After thirty-eight days of strenuous climbing, countless long leader falls and thirty-five pitches of state-of-the-art climbing, Todd Skinner pulled himself over the top of the Salathe Wall of Yosemite's El Capitan. He and Paul Piana had free climbed one of the longest and most difficult routes anywhere and it was time to celebrate. But fate did not allow it and a moment of exultation instantly turned to terror.

When Royal Robbins, Chuck Pratt, and Tom Frost first climbed the Salathe Wall in 1961, it was hailed as the greatest rock climb in the world. Piana and Skinner believed that the quality of the route was high, and that given good weather, good health, and enough preparation, they could become the first to climb the entire route without using pitons or chocks for direct aid.

"This was the best goal I could ever imagine," explained Skinner. "If we could climb the Salathe Wall free, it would eclipse anything that I have ever seen. But it is 3,600 feet high and all it takes is a five-foot blank section and suddenly it won't go free. It doesn't matter if it almost goes. Even if we freed all but five feet and made one aid move, that would be a failure."

Skinner climbed the entire route twice looking for such a spot. He talked with others who had the same idea. "Stefan Glowacz [a leading German climber] made two strong attempts on it and he said one part would never go free and another part would go, but it would take ten years before anybody would be good enough to do it. It didn't sound good, but it was a shining goal."

The two trained all winter and arrived in Yosemite in top co... were ready to start climbing but didn't know where to begin on such a project. The steepest sections are on the last pitches. They considered rappelling from the top to try those out, but decided to start low and work up. If they found that elusive blank section, the climb would be over and they would stop.

"We would go up for five or six days and come down for a day, go up for five or six days and come down," Skinner explained. "We fixed ropes but not all the way up. We had about ten ropes fixed and when we were working on Pitch Seventeen, which was a very hard one, we fixed the ten ropes, climbed the other pitches and lived up there. All in all, we spent thirty-eight nights on the wall and another ten days hauling water up and coming back down the same night."

Many of the pitches had been free climbed by various climbers in the past, but two pitches had not. These most difficult pitches were in the top five in the vertical headwall area.

"Nobody thought that the headwall would go free," Skinner recalled. "We started with the pitch right over the roof, which was 5.13b. Then we had a long pitch, an enduro nightmare of 5.13a. The next pitch was technical, powerful 5.13b. Right before these three pitches were two pitches of 5.12, so this was a tremendously sustained section of climbing."

In practicing each of the pitches, the pair had to work out some unusual strategies. They filled cuts in their hands with Super Glue. And because of the number of pitches and the intricate nature of the handholds ("most of the time we had a ten percent chance of our hands staying in the crack"), they used blackboard chalk to draw symbols on the wall, giving clues as to the position of each hand and foot. Sometimes arrows pointed to blind placements or indicated if a hand was placed thumb up or down.

"The logistics were disgusting," Skinner remarked. "To work on a pitch we had to sometimes climb 2,000 feet to work on a ten-foot section. We did all our own hauling and we had hundreds of pounds of gear. The whole wall looked like a football play because you can't remember that many 5.12 moves. We memorized each piece of protection and had them in order, marked, and knew which hand to take it off the rack with."

After twenty-six days of working on the difficult sections, they had free climbed every single pitch. Now came the major challenge—to free climb them all from the ground up in sequence.

"When we started up for that final push, I was giving us a fifty-fifty chance. Nobody, including us, had ever done so many pitches back to back at such difficulty. We were fortunate that we didn't hurt a finger. It was cool, actually cold, which was to our advantage. Three days of rain would have been the end of us. Time was so important that we had to keep climbing. You couldn't take the days off that you needed badly. Everything was just perfect."

Until the last moment.

"At the top of the thirty-fifth pitch, Paul had anchored us to a massive block, as big as a fireplace. I got to the ledge and he was hauling up the bag. I was helping by pulling up on the weight of the bag while he pulled up the rope. The bag hung

...d Paul pulled hard and I pulled up. Suddenly, the
...ping us off the rock. It never fell down, it just slid off
...l's leg, slid across it and twisted it.

...n the haul, Paul had clipped himself into some extra pitons.
...d, I took two or three steps to try to get out of the way. A
...my back and the rock crushed me against the rope tied to the
...smashed for a second, but then the rope broke and freed me and
free... who was tied to it, thank God. I flew off the edge and hung just below it. The ...ck teetered and fell like a building over the top of me and cut the rope behind me. I was pinned there for a second. Paul thought I went all the way down, because he looked and all he saw were rope ends.

"This was the freak part of it. The rock had cut two ropes to the right of mine and one to the left. It had also smashed my ascender right at the lip where the others were cut. But fortunately, my ascender wasn't six inches higher or lower. It was right where it had to be so that this thing wouldn't cut my rope. It cut the others so cleanly they were melted. They were cut and sealed. Some were cut in ten places. They were diced.

"Our haul bag was cut off and fell 3,600 feet to the ground. Paul's legs were smashed and he saw me go over the edge and thought I was gone. Then he said he saw this bloody hand grab the ascender. I couldn't breathe—I just pulled myself up and lay there on my side coughing.

"We sat there for forty-five minutes and started freezing. We were in our T-shirts and we had nothing left. It cut loose everything from matches to coats to food and water. It was all gone. We sat there a long time wondering what to do. Paul's leg was bleeding pretty badly and, as it turned out, was broken in four places. Finally, I could breathe and realized that I wasn't going to die. It took me half an hour to stand up. We knew we weren't going to be rescued, but we also knew we couldn't live through the night. We found enough rope scraps to make the rappels. You usually have to make three, but we had to make seven because we didn't have a full rope. It took us about seven and a half hours to crawl down.

"I had two broken ribs, but that wasn't the worst part. I had pulled a muscle off the tip of my hip. I couldn't lift my leg and extend it in front of me. It was grim. When I started walking, I urinated every three or four minutes. I got scared because that is not normal. The doctor said it was just stress on the kidneys.

"That was a funny end to a brilliant route. It was wild because that was the top. Not only were we at the top, but our haul bags were up, too. We were there. We were off the route. As the first haul bag came over, we were laughing wildly. We spent over fifty days dreaming of this and we were going crazy and suddenly the celebration of success on the most unlikely project we ever dreamed of changed to a celebration of simply being alive."

The dream of free climbing the Salathe Wall had come true. It had taken five pitches of 5.13, ten 5.12's, and another several 5.11's, and had almost taken their lives. Perhaps the Salathe Wall, for a second time, could be called the greatest rock climb in the world.

Long, strenuous rock climbs are not the only dream Todd Skinner has had.

He dreamed of putting together the first American team to participate in the Russian Speed Climbing Championships and pulled that off, as well.

With teammates Beth Wald, Russ Clune, and Dan Michael, Skinner not only participated in the competitions, but brought home three bronze medals. "It's a valid competition," he asserted, "even though speed climbing is an empty skill. It has no application anywhere else.

"Thousands of people come to watch and millions watch on television. They have a series of national competitions and they are followed all over the nation, like we follow football or skiing.

"When we got there, we didn't even know the rules. While we were warming up, an interpreter read four pages of fine print to us. We still don't know all the rules." He laughed. "We watched other people to learn what we had to do.

"They held a stop watch on you and had a countdown in Russian. When you started, they had two guys doing what we called the Russian Spence Tracy Belay." He laughs. "These two big guys with mittens grabbed the rope and as you climbed they would hand over hand the rope, trying to keep up with you.

"Since we were the first Americans, we were a novelty. They were trying to trade us out of everything. People were selling carabiners for twenty-five dollars and Lycra pants for ninety dollars. Who knows what we could have gotten for shoes? That was as much fun as any of the climbing. They also have a funny custom—instead of asking for autographs, they give them."

On another foreign trip, Skinner picked up a geology book in Israel. He looked through it and found some interesting formations, but the book was in Hebrew, which he does not read. He asked someone to translate and learned the rocks were on the Sinai Peninsula.

"We did new routes on Mt. Sinai itself and we camped there for forty days just for that purpose. We did wild climbs—crack climbs mainly on Joshua Tree-type domes on a Yosemite scale. We did tons of new routes there because no one else had ever been there and the domes were really close together.

"Naming those routes was really fun. One route we did on Mt. Sinai we named The Infidel." He laughed. "We had a beautiful corner we called the Glorious Koran and we named another one Wind and Sun and Sword, which is the translation of a Bedouin chant."

To climb at the level he does, Skinner has developed an extensive training system. He explained, "We talked to a lot of human anatomy people, especially at the University of Wyoming, trying to isolate which muscles we use doing what. We developed a gymnasium that applies that. We wear weight jackets to amplify the gravity. When we are just doing pullups, I wear sixty pounds. I think it's really important to hold right here [he bends his arm ninety degrees at the elbow, as if in mid-pullup] so I made a ladder and I pullup as slowly as I can. I wear a twenty-five-pound jacket when I do that. It's really a series of one-arm pullups. Then coming down, I hold as long as I can. At first, I could barely slow down and now I can hold for forty-five seconds with no weight jacket. This helps when you don't have your feet on anything solid and you're holding on with one hand and ripping through your rack with the other.

"We also made a box—they jokingly call it the Skinner Box—that helps a lot on overhangs. You crawl in it like a cage and pretend you are doing roofs with your feet level with your hands. You put on lots of weights and pull up with your feet up. Then you lower down and pull up and lower down. We also have a fingertip ladder that I cut out of a four by four. We try to make these things as specific as possible.

"We're building more strength than we need. It's all overkill. Half of it is to convince yourself that you are strong. There are a lot of people that are strong if they would believe in their strength. I know a guy so strong he can hold an Iron Cross [on the gymnastic rings] for ten seconds. He can do ten one-arm pullups with each arm, but he can't climb nearly as well as a lot of other people. Somewhere a connection goes out. If he could apply that strength, he'd be better than anybody. I think the formula comes out eighty-five percent mental, ten percent physical, and five percent something beyond, something that kicks in occasionally, that is assistance from somewhere else, the ozone." He laughs. "It's a spiritual lessening of gravity or something. You know your mind couldn't help you, your strength couldn't help you, and something else kicked in and you faked it for a few moves.

"Everybody I know right now who is climbing at this level is training like this. Now, 5.12 is becoming accepted as will 5.13 eventually. Just a few years ago, 5.12 was absolutely out of control. Perhaps the workout isn't all of it, but you are getting away from the guy who can just naturally do hard climbs. I think that breaks off at about 5.10 +. You are getting people who are so dedicated to training these small, isolated, but most significant muscles that they will be able to have the mind to apply it and they will blow the standards away again. Every five or six years, there has been a blowing away and an acceptance of another level. I don't think we're even seeing the limit. It's starting to get away from the masses. The parabola is starting to shoot like that [he pointed up] and maybe only one or two guys in the world are going to be the level. It's just going to be a spearpoint that we can't even imagine now. Just like they couldn't imagine 5.12 back in the sixties, we can't imagine what's going to come up.

"There's a route in California that took 110 climbing days and it's rated 5.13c. He [Tony Yaniro] built a model of the crux. He took calipers up on aid and built a wall with this climb. He measured the exact size of the holds and distance between them and with what angle. The next guy came along and climbed it in eight days. It's going to be that a guy has a project that is going to take him years and it's also going to be that nobody will repeat it because anybody that could repeat it will have a project of their own. Why train so hard to repeat somebody else's route? Why not find your own and be known for that? It's going to be longer and longer times between first and second ascents of the hardest routes. It will come to the point where your name will be synonymous with say 5.14 +. And that may take your entire climbing life to do that. This is a sub-sport. This isn't even rock climbing anymore.

"You can't keep climbing this intensely for very long. People start burning out. They quit climbing. They don't drop back down in levels—they quit. I think there is just one day when you can't do it anymore. In climbing, the heroes, the head-liners, are short-lived. The people that are the absolute best, the top of their sport, next year, perhaps, won't be known by young climbers.

"However, you are gaining some sort of eternal recognition because every climb can be done the first time only once. It will live longer than you. We know Robbins's routes. Chouinard's routes are famous. And they are known not only for being good routes, but they're known for being Chouinard's and Robbins's routes. Long after we stop being an entity, people will come and climb the Skinner routes and know them as that. We may stop performing, but our performances will last."

It seems odd perhaps to call a climb a performance, when that word implies an audience. In rock areas near cities, climbers do sometimes draw a crowd, but more often than not, the audience is only a ropemate. Sometimes even that person is absent.

"You think of the huge crowds of people who show up to watch a football game, massive crowds that just go crazy watching a sport where, at the very worst, a team is going to gain less points than another. Then you think about some horrendous solo climb where a guy has trained his mind for years and there is nobody at all. If I solo, and I like soloing more than leading or top roping or anything, I don't want anybody to watch, because it's absolutely a personal thing. I'm afraid that if anybody is there at all, any single move or partial move might be made with them in mind. If you're soloing at the razor's edge, you're performing at the ultimate level where, if you make a mistake, you die.

"The climbing and soloing aren't worth dying for, but they are worth risking dying for. That's the same thing as high-stakes poker. If you're just playing for matchsticks, the excitement is gone, but what more can we add to a game than the ultimate? You're putting in everything you have. Everything becomes trivial, then, except for perhaps ten hard moves in a row five hundred feet off the ground. There's nothing more intense. Nothing at all. All we have is climbing shoes and a chalk bag. I don't even take pieces [of protection] in case I need them because that lessens it. I could plug in a Friend and hang on it when I'm just about to die.

"I've soloed 5.11's and there are some 5.12's I would solo. I've soloed 5.10's without having climbed them before. It adds more intensity. Who knows what's going to be around the next roof?

"You divorce yourself from reality on a solo. Never can you imagine yourself falling. You don't. You have separated yourself from mortality, so to speak. When you finally die soloing, it's going to be from something you couldn't control, like a hold breaking or a rock hitting you or something like that, but when you are on the climb, you don't think about dying. You don't try to force yourself not to. You just don't.

"I don't just solo, because I like to be able to fall on really hard climbs. When you're soloing, you don't have the option of falling and trying it over and over again. Having a rope allows you to step further and further into pure difficulty. You've eliminated the ante. If you do fall, even long falls, you live.

"I think a lot of my future lies in protected climbs, but facing huge falls where [if you fall] you are going to fall a hundred feet, but you are not going to die. That is sometimes why we solo, because then it feels so reassuring to have a piece anywhere or even just a rope. Some of these new routes don't seem to protect well and maybe we won't protect them. Maybe we'll just work the moves out. I've sometimes done this on purpose, where I could have protected something with a piton and I've not done it, partly for myself because the first-hand experience of having gone through that is valuable and, secondly, so that you can scare other people." He laughed. "You know that anybody else that gets on it is going to be gripped. So that's a monument not only to your strength, but to your head under duress."

Even though Skinner climbs nearly every day of the year, he observed, "We don't have to climb. You realize that pretty soon, if even subconsciously, that the making of moves on rock is a weird thing to think about. Why do people spend time, money, effort to touch a rock and move up it? They are in search of something else. I chose this because I have analyzed as many sports as I could, and I realized that people look for the key in most sports and here we've been given the key. Now we look for the door. I don't know if we're a step ahead or if we're transdimensional, but now, we're looking for the door with the key. The door, well, we know that it probably opens inward, but other than that, we're looking for something that we know we'll never find. Some people are disillusioned when that becomes a conscious thought, when they realize that they are not going to find what they are looking for in a sport. Other people, realizing that, know that whatever the trials they are going to go through looking for it, it will be so sweet that it's worth years in the searching."

Glossary

Aid Climbing   Climbing in which progress is made by using pitons, chocks, bolts, or other devices for supporting body weight. Used where free climbing is extremely difficult or impossible.

Aiguille   A needle-like rock mass or mountain peak.

Alpine Style   Method of climbing on big mountains in which a party moves up the mountain carrying all their gear with them rather than leaving stocked camps. This usually means lighter and faster ascents, although the danger is often increased.

Belay   An anchor to which the rope is attached, or the act of protecting a climber by using the rope.

Bolt   A metal device that is secured by drilling a hole in the rock and hammering the bolt through a hanger, a loop of metal that allows carabiners and other equipment to be held to the bolt.

Carabiner   A metal snap link with a spring-loaded gate. Usually oval or D-shaped. Used for many purposes in attaching a rope or piece of equipment to a piton, bolt, or other anchor.

Col   A saddle between two peaks.

Cornice   An overhanging lip of snow formed on the leeward side of a ridge or summit. They pose danger to a climber because they are not often visible from above and may break under the climber's weight.

Couloir   A glacier-carved gully.

Crampon   Set of steel spikes that are attached to the bottom of a boot for firm footing on snow and ice.

Crevasse   Hole in a glacier formed by the ice breaking as it moves over uneven bedrock. Potentially dangerous to a climber if the crevasse is covered with snow and is not visible. Thus, climbers often rope together on glaciers, even when walking on flat terrain.

Crux   The most difficult part of a pitch or climb.

Dead man   An aluminum plate that is buried in a snow slope to provide an anchor point. It attaches to the rope by means of a cable and carabiner.

Enduro New wave climbing slang for endurama: a long, sustained, difficult pitch of climbing.

Exposure The amount of open air beneath a climber on a climb. This affects the mental side of climbing and the climber's willingness to make a move.

Figure 8 One of many friction devices used to control the descent while rappelling on a rope.

Free Climbing Climbing style that emphasizes using only naturally occurring handholds and footholds, and which avoids using climbing hardware for support or progress.

Friends A mechanical point of protection with four cams that work independently to allow the device to expand and contract to fit varying sizes of cracks. May be used for protecting a lead climber or as part of a belay anchor.

Ice Axe A tool used in climbing on ice and snow. It has a sharp pick and a broad adze, which make it useful as a moveable handhold for both securing a climber and for chopping or digging. On steep snow, the axe may also be used to stop a fall in a move known as a "self-arrest."

Ice Screw A metal spike that is driven or twisted into ice to protect a lead climber or form an anchor.

Jug Slang term for using a jumar to ascend a rope.

Jumar A camming device that will move up a rope, but not downwards. Used on difficult climbs to protect a climber by allowing him to move upward, but not fall. On vertical rock or ice, a climber may also literally climb the rope using two jumars and slings for footholds. This term is also used as a verb meaning to use a jumar.

Nut A metal wedge that is inserted into a crack to protect the lead climber. A carabiner attaches the rope to the nut and lets the rope move upward as the leader progresses.

Pitch One rope-length or less of climbing after which the leader stops to belay his partner.

Piton A metal spike that is hammered into a crack to protect a climber or provide an anchor.

Prusik A sliding knot made by wrapping a smaller rope around the climbing rope in such a way that unweighted, it will slide upwards, but under a climber's weight, it will constrict and stay in place. Used for ascending a rope; has been largely replaced by the jumar. The term is also used to describe the process of ascending by using this method.

Rappel Means of descending a rope by use of friction devices or carabiners to control and slow the descent.

Roof A horizontal overhanging section of rock.

Suggested Reading

Blum, Arlene. *Annapurna: A Woman's Place*. San Francisco: Sierra Club Books, 1980.

Bonington, Chris. *Everest the Hard Way*, New York: Random House, 1976.

_____. *The Everest Years*. New York: Viking Penguin, Inc., 1987.

_____. *I Chose to Climb*. London: Victor Gollenz, Ltd., 1985.

_____. *Kongur*. London: Hodder and Stoughton, 1982.

_____. *The Next Horizon*. London: Victor Gollenz, Ltd., 1976.

_____. *The Quest for Adventure*, New York: Crown Press, 1982.

Chouinard, Yvon. *Climbing Ice*. San Francisco: Sierra Club Books, 1978.

Cleare, John. *The World Guide to Mountains and Mountaineering*. Exeter, England: Webb and Bower Ltd., 1979.

Cleare, John. *Mountains*. New York: Crown Publishers, 1975.

Cobb, Sue. *The Edge of Everest: A Woman Challenges the Mountain*. Harrisburg, Pa.: Stackpole Books, 1989.

Conn, Herb, and Jan Conn. *The Jewel Cave Adventure*, St. Louis: Cave Books, 1981.

Ferber, Peggy, ed. *Mountaineering: The Freedom of the Hills*. Seattle: The Mountaineers, 1977.

Gregory, John Forrest. *Rock Sport: Tools, Training, and Techniques for Climbers*. Harrisburg, Pa.: Stackpole Books, 1989.

Houston, Charles, and Robert Bates. *K2 The Savage Mountain*. New York: McGraw-Hill Book Co., 1954.

Jones, Chris. *Climbing in North America*. Berkeley: University of California Press, 1976.

Lyman, Tom, and Bill Riviere. *The Field Book of Mountaineering and Rock Climbing*. New York: Winchester Press, 1976.

Mitchell, Finis. *Wild River Trails*. Salt Lake City: Wasatch Pub., 1975.

Moore, Terris. *Mt. McKinley: The Pioneer Climbs*. Fairbanks: University of Alaska Press, 1967.

Muir, John. *The Yosemite*. San Francisco: Sierra Club Books, 1988.

Rebuffat, Gaston. *On Ice and Rock and Snow*. New York: Oxford University Press, 1971.

Ridgeway, Rick. *The Boldest Dream*. New York: Harcourt Brace Jovanovich, Inc., 1979.

_____. *The Last Step: The American Ascent of K2*. Seattle: The Mountaineers, 1980.

Ridgeway, Rick. *Seven Summits*. New York: Warner Books, 1986.

Robbins, Royal. *Advanced Rockcraft*. Glendale, Calif.: La Siesta Press, 1985.

_____. *Basic Rockcraft*. Glendale, Calif.: La Siesta Press, 1971.

Roberts, David. *Moments of Doubt*. Seattle: The Mountaineers, 1986.

Roper, Steve, and Allen Steck. *Fifty Classic Climbs of North America*. San Francisco: Sierra Club Books, 1979.

Roskelley, John. *Nanda Devi*. Harrisburg, Pa.: Stackpole Books, 1987.

Rowell, Galen. *Alaska: Images of the Country*. San Francisco: Sierra Club Books, 1981.

_____. *High and Wild*. San Francisco: Sierra Club Books, 1979.

_____. *In the Throne Room of the Mountain Gods*. San Francisco: Sierra Club Books, 1977.

_____. *Many People Come Looking, Looking*. Seattle: The Mountaineers, 1980.

_____. *Mountain Light: In Search of the Dynamic Landscape*. San Francisco: Sierra Club Books, 1986.

_____. *Mountains of the Middle Kingdom: Exploring the High Peaks of China and Tibet*. San Francisco: Sierra Club Books, 1983.

_____. *Vertical World of Yosemite*. Berkeley: Wilderness Press, 1974.

Scott, Doug. *Big Wall Climbing*. New York: Oxford University Press, 1974.

Sheehy, Gail, *Passages*. New York: Bantam Books, 1977.

Smith, George Alan, and Carol D. Smith. *The Armchair Mountaineer*. New York: Pitman Publishing Corporation, 1968.

Stuck, Hudson. *The Ascent of Denali*. Seattle: The Mountaineers, 1977.

Ullman, James Ramsey. *Americans on Everest*. Philadelphia and New York: J.B. Lippincott Co., 1964.

_____. *High Conquest*. Philadelphia and New York: J.B. Lippincott Co., 1941.

Magazines:

American Alpine Journal, 113 East 90th Street, New York, NY 10028.

Climbing, P.O. Box E, Aspen, CO 81612.

Mountain, P.O. Box 184, Sheffield, England S11 9DL.

Rock and Ice, P.O. Box 3595, Boulder, CO 80307.

Summit, 111 Schweitz Rd., Fleetwood, PA 19522.